S0-CAI-360

IT MIGHT DO WELL
WITH STRAWBERRIES

DAVID MATLIN

MARICK
PRESS

Library of Congress Cataloguing in Publication Data

Matlin, David
It Might Do Well With Srawberries

ISBN 10: 1-934851-02-7
ISBN 13: 978-1-934851-02-9

Copyright © by David Matlin, 2009
Edited by Elizabeth Myhr
Design and typesetting by Sean Tai
Cover design by Sean Tai
Cover photo by Ian Tadashi Moore

Printed and bound in Canada

Marick Press
P.O. Box 36253
Grosse Pointe Farms
Michigan 48236
www.marickpress.com

Distributed by spdbooks.org

For my friend
Angus Fletcher

Sections of this book have been published in *Mandorla, Notre Dame Review, The New Review of Literature, Golden Handcuffs Review, Fiction International* and *The Raven Chronicles.*

ACKNOWLEDGEMENTS

I would like to thank the following writers and editors for their generous support, Lou Rowan, William O'Rourke, Roberto Tejada, Douglas Messerli, Harold Jaffe and Phoebe Bosche. Most especially I would like to thank Ilya Kaminsky for his enthusiasms and aware suggestions and Gail Schneider for her fine critical eye.

In late June of 2006 I crossed the Richmond Bridge on the way to visit friends in Larkspur, one of the quiet bedroom communities in Marin County. No matter what high or low ground might be your choice in this village you can see Mount Tamalpais and the dry hills which surround this small mountain filled with the mysteries of its meadows, ravines, forests, wild flowers, ancient oak and redwood groves, coyotes, birds, rattlesnakes and swamps. It is also a world of sudden change where in a matter of minutes a steep, sun broiled trail can turn into a fog shrouded and uneasily misted semi-darkness accompanied by chilling coastal winds. The varieties of textured light and shadow, the fog banks carrying their scents of oak, sage, ocean spray, bird shadows, secret glen perfumes make this place seem at once a soothing and treacherous garden luring one to a lifetime of study and discovery though the tidy ever more peculiar early 21st century suburbias with their million dollar and more homes stacked into earthquake vulnerable hillsides are a force of almost parasitic abandon. The bordering wildernesses seem edgily awkward as the hot late afternoon winds rise up abruptly out of a sycamore darkened arroyo.

There is also an other wilderness one can see from these heights: San Quentin, the venomous, and according to our most precious and nuanced senses of post modernist ironies, ancient Hell House, as easily seen and inaccessible as Mount Tamalpais. One of the friends who we were visiting comes from a first settlement family in Bakersfield. Her great grandfather walked from St. Louis, and the shores of the Mississippi, to the shores of the perilously wild Kern River in 1857 as that water then burst out onto the San Joachin Valley floor from its remote birth pools in the Sierras. San Quentin Prison was already five years old. The birth of that California which begins with Sutter's Mill and the birth of this prison are inextricable. If it weren't for the fact that 6,000 inmates are caged here with 1500 civilians to manage "clientele" with an annual budget of $120,000,000.00 with the largest number of death row residents in the nation this would be the Bay Area's prime real estate merging the modern hungers for "development" with prison expansion. (The term "prime real estate" must be defined anew. On June 11, 2008 a series of facts were published in the Los Angeles Times about the expansion of a new death row housing unit at San Quentin. Though ground has never been broken construction costs have exploded by 80% since the authorization for the compound in 2003. Original projected costs: $395 million for 768 cells rather than 1,024 as first planned. Original projected cost per cell: $515,000.00. That cost has more than doubled to over $1,300,000.00. A death row prison cell of 4 ½' X 10' @ over $1,300,000.00 demands a new kind of real estate mythology in order for such bare-faced phantasmagoria to be, at best, even partially comprehended).

One can take the ferry to San Francisco and have a kind of ring-side seat where you can see individual "inmates" in outdoor cages. You could say that might be one hell of a jittery ride but the local citizenry has grown so accustomed that these scenes of torture seem normal and the horizon of the wider citizenry which so easily resides in the "Three Strikes Law" seems to take comfort and solace in such images. The prison is huge and looks like a permanently anchored cruise ship with its bow and stern sliced off by a cutting torch. The thing looks fog-eaten, fantastically rotten in its lifelessly certain dull weight, and its promise to invade all of our futures for centuries. When I see our version of ziggurats I often feel that no woman or man born can look long at these objects without being converted to their evil. Though this may be the core of story in so much of our art the assumption of innocence is as sneaky in me as it is anyone else; stare or not it doesn't matter; the theft and its acids have poured over us.

I've thought a lot about that "solace" we have embraced and what it means to me personally and what it might mean for my Nation. The "acids" I refer to are Guantanamo, Abu Ghraib, Bangram, the Black Sites wherever they might be and the civil disintegration we so expertly manage in "the Homeland" as if it were a dairy herd. This book is a commentary on that "solace." Its focus is the years 2004 and 2005. In this twenty-four month period phenomena appeared which no previous human generations have experienced.

Who are my days? This question haunts the core of these writings. And hovering over this two-year space lies another question which has to do with Whitman and what the Nation belongs to and whether we as citizens can any longer belong to the nation in what it is letting itself become. The daily facts as they are recorded here come mostly from the New York and Los Angeles Times. A wandering about, searching as I could, for some means of expression before what has so bewilderingly numbed and silenced. How could I as one person speak exactly as I can before that numbness and what it has and continues to mutilate. The mutilation is much more astute than it has ever been. The empire of that astuteness and how it has expertly immersed our lives in a radical disarray and a bigotry against humane accomplishment are what this book attempts to speak to. That bigotry has risen before but never in a time so delicate as this and so filled with a contempt for the cold, mysteriously awful Safe Conduct which helps us as Creatures to imagine a Life Courage and Desire to be Alive. How do any of us face the " . . . condition," as Pasternak said "by which the whole of reality has been seized . . ." Against that seizure I try in these recordings to speak to the smallest rituals of daily life, daily care and loving as I know them. To forget these "minute particulars" as Blake knew in the crisis of his world is to fall into a purgatory where the "lapsed soul" can no longer hear it own call: "O Earth O Earth return!" A wish so simple, and to Belong to, out of which a Song of Experience might begin.

As I return to this preface in late December of 2007 the prison budget for the State of California has bloated by 79% since 2003. What does this number mean? Since 2003 the prison population has increased by 8% to far more than 173,000. The yearly cost for prisons has jumped from $8.5 billion to over $10 billion in just four years. Included in this is a 6% annual increase in prison spending for the next five years. The spending also calls for a $7.5 billion borrowing increase for more prison space because of catastrophic overcrowding and the collapse of the prison health care system causing death through neglect and incompetence of at last two prisoners per week. That system has come under federal receivership and must be restored to Constitutional standards of well being most especially for those so easily despised who also come from families and communities. The cost of this neglect: a 263% increase in spending since 2000 or $2.1 billion per year. These numbers along with the rest of the numbers for each of the other states tell a story of neglect and a pageantry of hostility that has dulled us and allowed us the permission to gut our Constitution either stealthily or blatantly, it make no difference to the wonder/wreckage of our surround.

I've tried to do something different from my previous book "Prisons: Inside the New America from Vernooykill Creek to Abu Ghraib." There are various narratives, addresses to friends and family, fragments, poems, commentaries, observations, details about gardening, walking, reading, and daily joys with references to an earlier America, geography, pornography, geology, and the spectre of 17th and 18th century deep wilderness skinning camps out of which modern democracy began to emerge: the "Wrong Way Ophelia" as I've tried to imagine it in this time, her bones creasing the obscure Eno, Hico, and Haw rivers with the sense that the underlying poisoned sump of the prisons is only a scratch away. Upturn even the smallest dimension and one can smell its threat to our arts, our dreams, our tenderest daily cares. The terrible, stunning vocations of cruelty and stupidity are gathered and gathering in these months, staggering what is not and was never meant to be part of this human rapture.

The prisons have arisen in twentieth century Cold War Peacetime. When I consider this episode of modern democracy I recall Leslie Fiedler's "Love and Death in the American Novel" and the last pages of that unusually informative essay where the author cites the co-brutalities of twentieth century World War punctuated by twentieth century Peacetime which may have been arguably in its consequences at least as dangerous to planetary life as the unspeakably ghoulish and exhausting violences. The prisons are at the core of this paradox. What is the life of the artist before the fate of the nation in such a crucially fragile and delicate time?

I've taken the title "It Might Do Well With Strawberries" from one of Melville's strangest footnotes in "Moby Dick" at the end of "The Grand Armada." The incident and its terrible/marvelous enchantments has seemed to me since I first experienced it as young man in search of an art to be one of the necessary and disturbing whispers.

David Matlin, San Diego
2009

Trapezoid's weight of facial planes pulls the cheeks
flattens muscles around lips. Eye sockets
stretched by storms of miraculous hands carry the permanent sneer
of the butterfly's complex age in this woman of ancient Uaxactun engaged
in the first utterance of a verb designating the number Zero and its
relationship to the Moon and certain forms of Moon Death that once
sucked the "Sprout Name" out of Time. The formation of lips
triangular fingers ballooned by flood, urea, stopped-up kidneys.
The afflictions mark Her as half butterfly.
Her ugly, engorged limbs are about to burst
with what seems to be Creation/Disease but one can't precisely tell since
the glyph indicates the drowning of a nameless city in a sea of genital
blood spilled in panic by the rulers whoever they might have been.

The face is chewed by flower masked spiders.
The chin carries the deepest wounds.
Her clairvoyance is marked by toothed hummingbirds
and may be a "war event" recalling the looted identities
of the generations to come.

2005 (a splash of early January; weather cool and last night a chilling heavy mist descended). About the prisons in California and their connection to the destiny of a People, the Land, and the Life of the Land. The "Thing" has become the equivalent to an Atomic Age monstrosity swelled with its own growth principles of irradiated, compulsive, murderous permanence. No one has any idea about what to do or seems capable of humanely imagining what might be done other than some stuttery gropings that serve for either "explanation" or a kind of zodiac of helplessness fueled by the need to look tough on criminal justice for the elections now and the elections to arrive. Figure it was Vegas and those crystal meth cowgirls showing up in just their hats and boots on the edges of invisible radiation puddles offering instant leukemia for the lost and nuclear sinkholes with their arithmetic spread into the bloodstream offering a taste for the atomic and other disassemblies where large hilly land masses don't tend to increase air blast effects in some areas and lose them in others.

At the top of this food chain sits the California Correctional Peace Officers Union with its salaries, its dimensions of political control, its casting of itself into the legend of a "good deeds" enforcer. Here the sickness of the civilization with its care for deceit and the usages of the lineages of deceit finds the long sought for pure tyrannic respectability and its wonders of disgust ploughed up as what awaiting soil in Rimbaud's
   "Morning of Drunkenness"?

   Nothing is worn. No jewelry. Clothing. No sex.
   The L-shaped eyes might indicate a deeper vulnerability.
   That testicle, clitoris are branches of merely
   preparatory responses
   the surface of green jade can only begin to gather.

Despotism, oligarchy, democracy have become interchangeable totalities fed by constant patterns of planned for and mined disintegrations of particular populations and worlds whose traumas and exiles become idealized organs of retribution and the landscape of a more ancient America where, in the cauldrons of household afflictions, the ravings and ravers were born who caused the abandonment of cities.

The other two words used to describe the present phenomena at the core of our public secrets: "fatal" and "macabre." Punishment wedded to rupture and rapture zones, crater volumes, the lips at ignition a bi-curious daughter and mom rendezvous.

" ... Tell also of the False Tongue! Vegetated (Blake says in the opening passages to Milton: Book The First)
Beneath your land of shadows: of its sacrifices, and
Its offerings, even till Jesus, the image of the Invisible God
Became its prey ..."

In one instance at San Quentin Prison investigators watched a dentist for a whole day as he cleaned, checked, and did teeth of scheduled prisoners, without once changing his protective gloves or washing his hands. With the background of AIDS haunting these chambers of filth and murder such deliberate actions appear to be images of Death Carriers allowed to go back into their communities to infect wives and children into the American version of legal quietudes and contempts that devastate and permanently maim. Such savagery and violation, such depravity is the purchase of a People who are at the services of their secret barbarities and alliances with safety, security, and "morality" which has allowed and will continue to allow itself all the luxuries of abandonment which justify this form of extermination and breakage without one moment of doubt. I think of H.D.'s "still the Luxor Bee" and what reservoirs of visionary anguish that image might have held for her as a totem haunting the Life of America

and herself; the ancient material of the Nile, the Euphrates, the Tigris
stinging us, the proud inoculated unsuspecting moderns and the spell of
our inoculations having become a termite cloud about to finish its mating
flight on the horizon.

Who can swear
not to eat lungs
as the ancient Grandmothers
had once done?

Load up on wild rice
keep to yourself

as of a snow flake
whitening the ground

Does no life-sap
spread away then
in any of the seconds
calling to women
to men
before they can ever
call to themselves?

The quiet ugliness of the trespass
gossip over the ravening whirlpools
at the ends of the most secretly numbered days
of a final sex hunt
you can almost taste?

More ugly news from Iraq. Nothing learned about Abu Ghraib. The American occupiers have now a bursting population. What to call this in the actual language of the world which we now confront; ambient pressure, 58 generations of neutron release, the realizable temperature of H2 + H2 = He3 + n + 3.2 Mev designating the production of energy at the height of burst whether Abu Ghraib, Guantanamo, or the Los Angeles County Jail. "He" here is helium. His helium count is up today. There was deuterium in his piss; so much the nurses thought the son-of-a-bitch was gonna float out the fuckin door. Plutonium in his semen. Uranium so far up his asshole even the local preacher threw the church plunger away. MEV: Million electron volt units – ole Mev, she flipped her olds twice with the help of Jack Daniels stuck between her legs and jes kep drivin.

Thousands and thousands as if the whole world, the one outside of America's borders will end up as our "Detainees" – the word sewer here – at Abu Ghraib during the period of the revealed abuses the maximum number of prisoners was said to be 2,500. There are, as I write these number in late February of 2006 more than 10,000 clientele. Our will to New Jack a planet may be the "Rapture" in its form of an astrological frenzy masquerading as the single species option in search of planetary closure.

Option, a noun, sideways winding in the trees popped dead cold as a woman's broken egg thrown to the ants. Hard package. Pump it. Brain down. Figure this business is really really old something to do with early patterns of Homo Erectus women wandering in their hyena or jackel forms in their initial curiosities over what might lie beyond the hills and ravines of the Nile and about to emerge Great Rift Valley; the night labors of that lycanthropy signaling the migrations out of Africa. A million and-a-half, two million years ago?

As to the matter of food: time is hungry. The phrasings of its appetite are given as a descent where the nectars of fate are sucked. In this there are said to be demons who preside. One who was seen at the edges: "Xtabay,

Hanging Woman Demon" accompanying the American soldiers out of the previous prophecies as an interrogator in Afghanistan before murdering an Afghan Detainee sold into confinement by a local warlord, who was said to have placed his penis along the face of his victim previously chained to a ceiling. There are reports of the Four Ancient Sun Giants from the American Jungles who also may have watched: the Pouah Tun defining these smallest incidents as "The Return of the Asshole Boils" naming the Beginning of a New Time. 10:00am, 60 degrees. Overcast. Thick, heavy raindrops falling, it seems reluctantly from a mothering sky. Vital nuclear bomb making components destined for Libya's nuclear weapons program have been missing since October of 2003. No one on the planet seems to know where these "components" and "specialized tools" are, but leads so far indicate Abdul Quadeer Khan's smuggling network. Khan traveled extensively and had contacts worldwide. Rotors are missing for P2 centrifuges for enrichment, as is high strength aluminum and maranging steel for centrifuge manufacture. The list also includes precision tools to produce fissile material for converting uranium ore into gas and then pumping it into thousands of interconnected centrifuges spun at twice the speed of sound to separate isotopes and uranium concentrate to produce the required materials for a single weapon.

How to regard the new hideous Sphinxs Shelley saw at the
Edges of the about-to-emerge world?
"Oh, write no more the tale of Troy,
    If earth Death's scroll must be!
Nor mix with Laian rage the joy
    Which dawns upon the free:
Although a subtler Sphinx renew
Riddles of death Thebes never knew."

And "Riddles": The "Laian" dream invasions have been abducted into the phrasings of new technologies: computer viruses, worms, multi-service operations, network fault management solutions, knowledge storms, network intrusion detection, e-mail security services, threat and vulnerability mitigation and in that this passage of Shelley's still reminds me of the American "Vision Serpents" with human torsos crawling half out of their mouths luring the creaturely consciousness of the living the breathing with the conch shells they hold in their hands, the ordeal of being swallowed by these beings, the demonic luxury and indolence emerging from their sacred spit and the concerts they are about to play for the regurgitated creatures of the trance cycles where Blue Hummingbirds sit in their yellow trees and are these the hallucinations brought about by population pressure, addictions to surgery in the upper classes, doubts about Botticelli's depiction of juvenile rheumatoid arthritis?

Skull Grandfathers, why have you left the imprint
of your feet on our faces?
Is this the ancient perch where the Butcher Beasts wait
for the throats, the eyes, the ears of all the born
worth ten thousand years of calories
per square second to the third power
As this Age we've become so soon heaps up
this museum of hard and soft targets
Calories per centimeter squared of Heat?
Who will speak once more?
Make the soil heave?
Stir the impulses needed, as Lawrence once said
"to smash the vast lie of the world"?

    Black as night
    is the food

but honey bees were
as were their red flowers

beneath these trees
these bushes
the vines beneath
which were once breadnut
and written as breadnut

Trees appeared, stone, Boiling War Carried in the Mouth
Tell us
Is that where we are going
Were we a someone
Perhaps a somewhere
Before the sounds of words leaked out
When Exhale was the Name of Heaven and Sky
And Inhale
Was the Name of the Birth of Night?

Be merciful, O Lord. Throw fingers soaked in the wells of virgins. Hell
with those pennies you reserve for wishful waters. What prayer to be said
before the about-to-be lovely wrongs we will suffer. The defoliations
before us reeking with defoliations to come irritable and smelly as shit
beetles rolling with their filthy quivering with worlds-to-come balls over
the hills of pre-Earth with its still smoldering tides. Those stink workers
pushing there. Their lined-up hordes collapsing the under-pendants of
uranium cliffs that didn't know ever if they'd become the atomic storms
loading the brain-pans of another species contest for desire and blood
poured by the by-the-clock Rocket Girls who really know the rules.
Pornography and time. Those Girls dripping over the clocks. Lips of
their cunts swelled with the secret powers of their animations to be

suddenly chocked out inside the instances of their wetting themselves over the helpless faces of impermanence and maybe a soaked pubic hair to drop randomly into the aching clouds of gasses that might or might not become worlds.

The marrow of Earth
    Burned
As the land is burned
    Cut as the Sky
Is cut
    And in a Beginning
One of the Thirteen
    So far to be counted

The Sun's eruption
    Resolved nothing
For the Born on that Day
    Who though they avoided suffering
Could do nothing
    But light the candle
By which suffering
    Would find its way
Back to them

God of 1.   Hunchback, eat.
God of 2.   Squat Face, drink.
God of 3.   Rising Storm, rain.
God of 4.   Rising Mountain, be the generation that hangs from trees.
God of 5.   Sooted Stump, keep stumbling in your ashes.

God of 6.   Shelless Snail, the slime of your foot; why does it drown
the hours?

God of 7.   Rolling Agave, what is the name of the mice who devour
your roots and who will set the seconds by their rotted
teeth?

God of 8.   Who melted your telephones?

God of 9.   Third Squeeze, why do you secretly fuck your pigs?

God of 10. Is it white for the death that accumulates there
and who can remember who watched over the eggs
of hawks?

God of 11. Three Hanging Sentences, who robbed your immemorial
nests and made you breathless?

God of 12. Old Bugger, which hole this morning for which pleasure?

God of 13. Many Guts, suggest an alternative, a distinction; snapshots
of pickle sandwiches or the memorizations of one of Allen
Ginsberg's news flashes:

> *I've been with an awful lot of beautiful*
> *juvenile delinquents. I've done my best*
> *to go to eternity with them.*

Foggy mornings with their vast mid-Pacific stench scratching at the profile
of seals watching him behind the water walls his shoulders or hips might
graze. He didn't know who committed the first murder of this version of
the Creation as long as this short didn't blow a piston between San
Bernardino and Vegas on a hundred ten degree night. He wanted to get
away from his friends who survived the bamboo vipered jungles only to
come back leak their brains against a freeway culvert because the Asian
coasts that cited their initiations produced the prettiest little rights and
lefts, soften even the hardest surfer's dream so he'd do some meth shine a
car think about the Crow warrior Crazy Sister-In-Law and how those

Horse Dreamers designed their twelve to eighteen foot locks let it flow behind them as they rode their animals over the flower scented oceans of land be damned careful about Oklahoma its skeletons of butchered Cheyennes displayed in front windows of local businesses whispering about Otto Preminger and his 1944 movie at least part of a female generation got named after that mood by which the women had to wait for men to die or live the raw absence of them left behind to spend days and years on the "Homefront" somehow boiled up into Gene Tierney and the mothers who'd name the daughters cast from their wombs the portrait of identities dispersed by the pronunciation birth notices sent to carrion mists at Bastogne or Iwo Jima to the legendary ballrooms on Catalina where Perry Como sang at least ten thousand of LA's finest coming-of-age girls out of their virginity and the marines oiling their obsolete M1s in the hills of Pendleton couldn't know exactly like those 30s maidens the extent of the ravishments about-to-be swaying over the continental basins and troughs the scale of it arching beyond the arch of the horizon some beautiful fin a previous world forgot to rot or the Cree who came every year to watch over him when he was a child had killed a bear with an axe when it came too close to the playpen on the edge of the woods and though the Cree was then an old man he'd stand on his hands walk like feet never existed teach him the rudiments of signs the stories and images made with fingers hands silently the ends of the body flickering this way in the air.

And is this the Portal of the Story
Are We the We in the nightmare of this Thirst

Who are this "We" in dream
the "We" to talk
thinking ourselves separate from talking
where thinking cannot linger

And who are the Dead?
Who causes the Sky to clear
all the way to the Marrow of Earth
in the account of words
planted in our walls?

And he was afraid to eat the avocado afraid it might mean he could eat the
father or the fathers drowned as if they were some foreign feather to their
own lungs luring the veins between their toes and hold the secret hungers
there against all the knowledge to come be slick too become snipers like
the World War II veterans in our desert towns who discovered themselves
on top of hills overlooking newly constructed freeways sighting their
scopes at torrents of steel below

                                                        strong   swift
      chest deep in death   where   the hummingbird   asks
                               for   no   quarter
             no   friends other   than the mind and hair

The State of California's corrections officials will scrap the centerpiece of
their effort to reform California's beleaguered parole system because there
is no evidence the new approach is working. Youth and Adult Corrections
Secretary, Roderick Q. Hickman, signed the memo rescinding this experiment so recently born so recently dead. The leaders of the California
Correctional Police Officers Association and various "crime victim"
groups are applauding this decision. The program was first put into place
by Governor Gray Davis in 2004 in the face of 67% recidivism rates for
adult prisoners. No data over this short period of time has been recorded
for either drug treatment programs or home detention with electronic
monitoring to discover if something, anything might work to avoid further
rush toward the fatalities we have embraced. In the place of even the most

meager attempt at clarity is the preference (in Melville's sense of the terminal, the suicidal) for setbacks such as contract disputes and delays in obtaining the monitoring devices. Each impediment evokes the fact that no one at the simplest level is capable of action other than a profound blockage that transmits disintegration, wreckage, and the codes of noise which enshrine these barriers.

I have wanted to say this is sorrow in the word's old sense of sickness and dread but that's too much a derivative or a too stale literary aesthetic; what we are examining is the luxuries of structural stupor and nothingness raised to a certainty similar to Edward Teller's "Project Plowshares" and the "Cold War" proposals to use nuclear weapons for civilian purposes; real estate and development schemes, flood control, and agriculture. The re-imaging of these vessels as implements of a new more homely dimension of the everyday residues released by underground blasts and the delicate glassware of that invisible production of a benevolence tinged with the exalted community and neighborly cravings for atomic fire. A farmer or weekend carpenter dreaming of such excited states may still be attached to his nuclei but within a hundredth or so of a microsecond will find that his atoms are stripped by the several tens of millions degrees pulsating either under the town or under the bathtub; a soft x-ray region where the Xibalbans paddle their canoes over the compression and steep fronted shock waves delighted by the creatures who, though they took two or three million years to do it, sometimes trying the patience of these Lords, did fulfill the expectations.

The falling "och be"
falls as only a verb can fall
Verb for Death is too
a sign of being
Carved on the Face of Rivers

There is a woman hacking a serpent with a hoe. The blade is sunk deep into the snake's back and her face as she does her labor is bathed in a twisted teeth crunched agony. Her left breast grazes her bent knee. The nipple is extended as the snake uncoils toward her unprotected labia. Dream terror marks the woman's eyes. Her nose is bulged with sexual discovery and desolation that has come to deliver and condemn her. Gourd bearing vines sprout from the hoe wounds. The serpent has a panther's head and her attack will begin the conversion of the monster's body into the yellow flowered gourd, ancestor of the pumpkin and other pumpkin-like squashes, their fleshy fruit descended from the terrible serpent being's meat. The woman also has a basket strapped to her back, one of the images of ferocious, sure women from the Mississippian Period which gave birth to Cahokia, site of the largest earth works in North America. Monk's Mound at its center is the third largest pyramid in the hemisphere, a hundred feet high with a base of thirteen acres. The Cahokians compacted different soils for each layer of their monument to minimize erosion. Such advanced engineering techniques mark this urban center and what would have been an extensive outlying agricultural complex. The Illinois, Missouri, and Mississippi Rivers join just above this Mississippian City which made trade, gossip, and transport of goods into their own down-range spinnerets penetrating far as Kansas, Wisconsin, Georgia, and Carolinas. Cahokians seemed too to like flint, the kind located still in the quarries of southern Illinois. They crafted a hoe that killed deep and made their city possible.

In the deeper forest some say there are vast towers
that they are ashen and spotted. Their smell ripe
on the winds that spread and fly and spiral.
There are people there who tell how those towers
whisper numbers and the numbers once said by those

towers wander in the forests around them searching
for duplicate pus of galaxies, loose teeth, the
the shifting noun written in the smoke the dead float upon

My contact with those long-gone others. What thinking was brought about them as each unstable, half corroded fragment appeared out of the dirt they may actually have stood on assumed a quietness for me, these stems from another world and their shadows as well as the stuff about the Chou and Shang. I studied the pottery of the older almost Neolithic people, how it moved toward elaborate finely poured bronze vessels of the Shang, first "advanced" civilization of China. The drama and mass of the pieces. I examined the materials for hours wanting to ask, my questions over the jade knives and burials, axe blades which seemed to me had been forged to cut off the heads of gods. My teacher spoke and read Chinese, was Quebec French, a scholar of Asia who said things about Vietnam, its history when asked, would describe a delta swamp or the daily routines of a northern villager. He was one of the earliest in those now faraway "Teach-Ins" to tell that America might kill a part of itself there and got publicly scorned down, his gentle unswaying revelations jeered. He would almost whisper about the Shang when I talked to him. Their metal technology, the delicacy and brutality of their transformation of rhinoceros and tigers into sound engorged bronze bells inlaid with silver and gold. It made me almost afraid to touch or smell the Pacific, my home Ocean.

The loom was small, hand-built, lying near a half-dried swamp.
Only in mid-summer would the one girl be allowed to go there,
pick wild raw cotton. Her tribe watched. Her steps were careful.
The rattlers huge, thick, sometimes twelve feet long.

If a girl was bit they'd wait another year, let the flesh dribble
that way, watch the pinkness of the bone go to dry white.
The swamp rose and fell gnawing at the luckless. If a girl went
there she'd see ribs, partially sinewed hands sunk in the areas
still holding stagnant water from spring floods.

The flox and honeysuckle bordered, holding a coiled, ready serpent.
The stands of cotton grew only here and here she'd pick, separate fiber
and spread seed for new growth for the new girls that must come.
When that was done she'd go to the loom.

Her raw cotton was considered a drip from the clitoris down to moisten
the labia. The loom waited. She'd spin readying the fiber. Her desire
for the oldest women tightening there, stretching before the ribs of the
other girls washed by the drying summer winds

Until 20,000 BC it was ice. In some parts estimated to have been fifteen
thousand feet thick. Ugly winds constantly blew down slope from a huge
dome centered over Hudson Bay at over a hundred miles per hour. Those
winds traveling to the margins of ice from southern Pennsylvania through
central Illinois and on into eastern Washington were target fixed on a g-
lock that bore straight into the life of the central continent. North America
at glacial maximum was covered by an ice sheet that has no comparison to
anything we might understand as severity. Where wind, ice, and earth met
there was both tundra and evergreen forest separated in a mosaic of tracts
by their mutual intolerance. What is now Michigan and Wisconsin, the
Dakotas and Montana, New York and Massachusetts, take any pick from
the deck, was crushed and sunk bedrock that saw neither light nor air for
a hundred thousand years until the start of the great melt which exposed
a zone at that beginning of a vegetation zero. The land at ice margin was

mostly permafrost wedded to the extremities of cold from Washington to New Jersey and casts of fossil ice wedges can still be found over this thousands of miles ancient border along with other symptoms of the disappeared sterilization where the southern-most ice froze and thawed at that surface until it rose into a near regular pattern of polygons. Such fossil earths can be walked over in Idaho or Pennsylvania at a hundred degrees above zero where nothing now might bite your toes but an over-persistent horsefly. The newly ice-free land was part frozen and then overwhelmed by tremendous lakes whose southern shores received pilgrim seed and pollen and whose northern reaches were glaciated cliffs calving icebergs that would begin their floatabout in one climate and going south melt in another. But it was the state of the ground that ruled. If it was permafrost, no forest. And such condition could have existed immediately after the ice's recession, or never for thousands of years. That new surface had had no organism growing in it, none walking on it and waited for the wind borne soils from the bordering unglaciated lands to become seed beds and nurseries and when those first plants died they composted and caused further wind-blown soils to accumulate. The story really can't begin without water and life of water. But there was another liquid too that came out of those Great Lakes systems. It was called "Willie Peter" and my uncles who'd seen it or sprayed it in one war and my friends who were doing the same in another would close their nostrils over the pronunciation of silent images rolling in their minds, say Lassen, Mona Loa, or Shasta couldn't pump hot death any better than the chemical giants who made that jelly. I was passing through Illinois while F-4s and F-5s were beginning a napalm experiment that'd gulp almost as much land and life as any long-term ice episode.

When the land heated and ran up against the relinquishing still hundreds of feet thick ice that covered Quebec and Labrador the war of temperatures caused dust storms that blotted the sun for weeks and months. There were no plants and the wind scoured and shifted all the top soils that would compost a later waiting world.

The rulers have come to an expertise, a threshold where reality has no substance, factual evidence to be abolished, and the living surface of our Daily Hold, Our Daily Belonging to a World transformed into an indeterminate, undermined parasite. Bush, Rice, Cheney; the sordid hemorrhage these people have mastered. There is in the background of these treacheries a strange image from the "Stardust Probe" – a comet ("Wild 2"), sharp, defined, spewing gas and debris, its tail a wash of organic molecules, carbon and nitrogen (the building blocks of life). A being so ancient, a wanderer who initiates Beginnings. Is it also the initiator of remnant debris from the Number Zero; the Dateless lying outside of time before the cycles began or one of the Tloque Nahuaque's primordial emissaries, Lord of the Near, Lord of the Close causing the decay orbits of memory and the disciplines necessary to make of that decay an evidence of mind shaping itself through ancient patterns of repetition as if the distance of a whisper might reassemble itself into Dawn as it was once known, the most political moment of the Day. Today too, it is reported in the New York Times, an atom underwent teleportation.

It was close on ninety degrees and I could see the Washita glowing in the sunrise. My mother packed me off in one of her convertibles. She'd wanted to tell about a Kiowa named Silverhorn. So we drove to Highland Park. The Southwest Museum was there and though that would mark her mind this foray was for something more important.
There was a strip of cloth she wanted me to see, hung on one of the walls. Silverhorn painted it and it was filled with fine teepees and horseshoe tracks and Seventh Calvary soldiers. They'd come in 1868. Hid behind the distantly elegant bluffs overlooking this river the two miles I was driving

from what's now Cheyenne Oklahoma and my mother thought if she and I could look at those pictures then she could release or lock her language away. For her it always came down to this western Oklahoma Valley, its aching discordant poise folding into the sky above it, or the Hill of Wild Peas. And the afternoon of June 25th 1876 was more than anything about the secret history of women in America. Custer and his men paused there to look at the huge village running alongside the Little Bighorn while their iron shod horses chopped up and shit all over everything. For the Sioux women that overlook was a place of deepest peace, fragile in late June and covered with flowers of ripening buffalo peas whose seed had been gathered and boiled for generations. The only thing that might harm the new sprouts were ants and jumping mice and anyway they seemed weightless as the Milky Way the way my mother had said it. And that Hill was the place of women's puberty dreaming for who could count how much of that female living and dying. It was a defilement, lost and crushed, now another nothing. Custer had been here at the Washita too, to attack mostly women and children, and the old in the depths of an ugly dangerous winter. It drove my mother near to dry tears thinking about those forgotten plops of horseshit and what they smothered. She spoke too about another River. One called the Pedernales and what was about to flow out of it. I didn't like my mother when she got like that. Maybe it's why I spent so much time in the Pacific trying to be a seal. One story she told me, among all the rest rising up out of that boiling American afternoon: two Cheyenne women who'd known of Custer's promise to the great Aorta Man, Stone Forehead, never "to harm the Cheyenne again," recognized the fresh killed body of this man; each shoved a sewing awl into his ears on into his head so that he could hear his own words once more. The favor done because of Mo-o-tzi, the beautiful young Cheyenne girl who bore Custer's child. It made him their relative, and rather than allowing the Sioux who wanted to mutilate his body for all the sorrow he caused, they cleansed him with this last act of mercy.

Three heads are worn ceremonially.
   One
      weighing down
                     the pelvic girdle
         is nearly fresh
         the nose intact
         eyes only
         just starting to rot

the lower jaw ripped away.

   The one at the throat is almost
   a perfect rectangle supposing
   a well of thunder stored in the larynx
   the God there box boned
   thick with the crisis of cells
   uprooting teeth

         eye sockets crunched
               to one plane

      marks the sinew
         across the once
fleshed jaw

The third
dressing the crown
is a Gila Monster its flayed head

      still alive dripping poison

            onto a hatchet

The figure   is   dancing   the   dwarfish

stunt of legs   misaligned   hips are a year

emeralds leaked from the flight of owls

She talked of other women who were not Indians who called their dusk
"Wolf Light" where all the destinies of women could be named and that
light before light was the necklace of the Womb Giants. What ocelots
would come to the shores of such stories and antelopes to sniff testicles,
vaginas, offer journey and return, fabulous harm – slavery before butterflies trained to fan clitorises of wanting women. Suck the hood and parted
lips. And where could I carry such telepathic debris?

God fingers   washing   livers
            In   mountain   streams

and there   were those who   sold dreams

                            vendors   in   streets

            grateful   for   business

He could see across to Canada. The smell of so much fresh water nearly
scared him. The water was lined with factories. Some made pharmaceuti-
cals but mostly it was cars, steel, rubber, and glass and the parts that made
them run and the people who fed the factories with at least three generations of themselves and their Eastern European neighborhoods. As he rode
this street he could see the transitions from workers' homes to the more

titled middle class houses constructed of red brick instead of clapboard and then the estates began, smaller at first and growing, each one claiming a segment of property bigger than the last. It was around four o'clock. The afternoon late day heat ground into the elms. Made their leaves droop. The mansion the cabby parked in front of matched the address he'd been given. He got out. Tied his hair in a pony tail. Touched the surfboard on his "T" shirt for good luck and walked toward the front door. The mother was in the middle of cocktails but maybe he could have walked backward the half continent he'd already come, at the end of it be a death hunter shrouded in the ways of ghosts and come to make everyone laugh before themselves. Do it in reverse. Close the gap between the world of the living and where the living go, make a spectacle of it, where we get sold off into madness and guessing games where no words for punishment ever exist.

           Path of blood in the body   Mare's-tail
               to tamp quiet   dangerous   bleeding

        (use as tea   for emergency clotting

                                 or chew   out   juice)

               Life and no
               running away

                                    Legs
                                    Throat
                                    Arms

            The Wells

Wind risen   above the knees above   the breast
No higher for the noon   spread of   air

The shadows of the dying sun touched the mansions, street after street of
them, the delicate engulfing leaves of the slowly diminishing light made
them seem frozen even harder in the courtship of results which spawned
their triumphs and frailties that could be traced to men in plumed hats
and silver buckled shoes who listened to the Ottawa, their stories of fresh
water seas and beaver waiting to be skinned by the millions, a cauldron of
ghosts and death and riches that would spew and possess everything lying
before it.

This city no matter his pedigree in it, forbidding as the old Fort, where
the Indians, the French, the peltry in beaver mixed with lead laced brandy
in a coma, slurping at the waves of desertions rimming the about-to-be
coldly treasured future.

There is a sad picture in the news today from the "Shinkolobwe" mines of
the Congo; a man in mindless exhaustion carrying a sack of cobalt, copper,
and uranium "soil" – the 1915 discovery when this was a Belgian colony
and which is also site of the original uranium used for the atomic bombs
dropped on Hiroshima and Nagasaki – this deadened wraith face; word-
less, unreal, fixed in the finalities of numbness – a hollow phantom carrying the ghastly treachery of Death Business at the core of the World. Death
Business which wants all and must be put to an end!
    "Shinkolobwe": is this the term that defines our time?
    No other seems to quite hold.
    No other term rises quite like this.
    Its sound so full of human origins and ruins.

Crazy Born "Co co al"
what does "rendition" mean
and are we a People
who mean to be the death of rain
before the bearers of the future arrive

This was a long time ago
in the middle of the Flower Sun
and Done
by the ancestors who were once flies.

Ghosts of the Split Word
Selling the Born
Your Pants
Your Clothes
You who are the weakness of this
stabbing bird's mouths
with borrowed houses

In the Navajo Mountain Chant the Singer sings
"In Life Unending, and beyond it." The opening
noun of the initial prepositional phrase begins at the
human foot and rises to fill the creaturely body.
Is this "Home" this "In Life unending" and
the "beyond it" is this "Home" too

and will it help us
to ask
Who prepared a City for a word?
Or a flowering meadow seizing a word
licking it like a woman licking her plate

        salty
    trusting the poisons

      And she is in your pants
        in your clothes
        in your words
        as a wasp brightening the land
        chased by swallows

Hear the Mohave wind as it picks up camel or pelican bones from its previous worlds joining the sounds of this world's arrangements.

    The ancient amusement. Trading fairs had taken place in America for thousands of years and Indians, even the most remote, came to stare at each other, buy each other's worlds from Lake Okeechobee to the Blue Mountains of the Walla Walla.

        Into this Old Fairgrounds Duluth formed a trading post
                        near

the Mississippi headwaters. He was interested in beaver. It was the same as oil or diamonds, big a gamble as roses in the Mohave that took my family to the shores of La Brea and the worlds in-waiting released by the bubbles there into the nameless surrounding air.

The fierce Plains warriors liked justice and bravery.

    Whichever

        Came up one-eyed Jack they didn't mind long as a speck of those alert darkened charms appeared on the borders where death and life make the teeth curl with the finery of the million lost and about-to-be. Duluth had done a rescue. Walked into a late seventeenth century camp of a thousand Sioux warriors to rescue the Franciscan, Louis Hennepin. They always seemed to recognize bravery and its dose of pure madness taking the wanderer to a canyon on Venus with its cliffs of ghost noises or the search for the "Vermillion Sea" where so many Europeans looked to get lost, get killed, get adopted into another humanity.

The lure of such wilderness, with its beaver patrolling an isolate pond, its translations into London or Parisian fashion in the seventeenth century. The women would look good in their powder and hair and false moles dazzling all the visitors who came to their bedrooms when bedrooms were really invented hung with bluest silk and the ladies in their fabulous beds before the young voyager found himself on the Plains with other voyagers' bodies in a precise circle separated heads wrapped in beaver pelt as notice of the hunger which brought them now vaporizing to such passage; the tribes trying in this way to satiate the new durations lying outside even their visionary guesses.

The money rested so lightly on her permeated
as it was with the severities and remove of a pastoral which made her
the shepherdess of what lay below, a
transporting serenity massive and soundless and without remorse
in either its custodial charities or its recesses
of contempt so the purchase of a small Matisse or Picabia, a plane trip
to bid on an eighteenth century Rocco chair
made a glimmering flood of seductions in their house but cold full of an
unapologized for nerve because she could mix
the European finery with a Crow bear claw necklace or a war shield
with white weasels hung from it for the dream
emergencies that appeared on the shores of the ancient Yellowstone
a treasure balanced on nothing more than the
sum of evaporations which clung to it and what it meant to personally

kill a grizzly for its human-like meat and oil
for insulation against buffalo gnats the toxic bites delivered over any
                    uncovered skin and what those white weasels
might say to the dreamer silent mercilessness of the small carnivores
                    come from the world of touchless mystery
where it invades the living no matter what shape the barren
                    transfixing nurture of it an almost unbearable
human extension its consuming repellence offering the dreamer
                    a comfortless fevered identity once lured
never to go away a hollow sky showing faintly its coiled pools
                    of noise the not-yet-lived produce
before the rustling of the one about-to-open eye among them
                    listening to Wyonnie Harris Little Willie John
but close stick your ear to Aretha Franklin specially the piano the singer
                    plays the back up melodies a co-dimension
inviting another foliage to come forward make you shiver even at the
                    beginnings of the hottest summer days
wanna be shrewd though pretend to be unyielding
                    and let the superficiality carry your uneasy
glances see nothing other than your entrance into the rightful
                    conclusions in waiting and promise me,
the one you know you'll break
                    take me for a dance.

Roses, come forward
        close your petals
    wait for sun
            to spread you
swell with hot waves of light

Mutilation begins at the crown of the sternum extending as a gouge straight down through the pelvic well. The meteor's furrow melted the soil that day, made a track the women thought was boiling semen. It made their nipples hard, hard laughter among themselves that flood shrunk to a mass of luscious going to decay injury flowering over the sore the earth comes to with no penetrant consolations for the lucky or unlucky.

> Suicide masters swallowing rainbows in empty rooms
> land of the poisoned sea
> eyes hanging from optic stalks
> for the Zero God to see through

I have been watching, each Sunday, in the last months, for the comic strip "Doonesbury" by Gary Trudeau. His "list" reminds me of one of Robert Duncan's writings about H.D.:

" 'The Tribute' is not an easy poem to appreciate in terms of what came to be accepted as H.D.'s virtues in the modern aesthetic of the twenties – the ardor kept in restraint, the Hellenic remove, the hard wrought art, the spare statement. The imagist rules will not fit. But once we turn from 'Cities' and the 'The Tribute,' keeping the contexts of these poems, the seemingly 'removed' Hellenism of 'Adonis,' 'Pallas,' or 'Sea Horses,' written in the same period, proves to be a screen image in which another level of feeling is present.

> *Akroneos, Oknolz, Elatreus.*
> *helm of boat, loosener of helm, dweller-by-sea*
> *Natueus, sea-man*

are lists of the war dead and lost from Homer. And now from our own sense of the experience of the War – and here her rites of remembrance

have quickened in us the impact of what happened before we were born –
we understand anew and in depth of agony of

> *But to name you,*
> *we reverent are breathless*
> *weak with pain and old loss*
> *and exile and despair*

"The individual in any given nation has in this war," Freud wrote in *Thoughts
on War and Death* in 1915, "a terrible opportunity to convince himself of
what would occasionally strike him in peace time – that the State has forbidden the individual the practice of wrong doing, not because it desired
to abolish it, but because it desires to have the monopoly of it..." as the poet
so frightfully cites the same on-going conduct for America.

And Trudeau letting the whisperings, irritations, and revulsions be woven
in, not to be denied or carted away.

Duncan's imagination of the "Strange Refusal" Freud saw at the core of
drastic trouble we are facing and have faced: "... for the crisis of the new
psychoanalytic wisdom lay in the resistance men have against knowing
what is above or below, the strange refusal to see what they are doing or to
hear what they are saying just when they are engaged in their own self-
destruction..."; but now Oedipus may be too thinned as story to reach for,
and though Duncan wanted to see in these "great compulsions" as he called
the symptoms, a "curious resemblance to the hubris and fate of the Greek
Drama" I see in these vocabularies, though their literary reference is very
attractive, more the underlying disruptions of the San Joachin Valley, the
"Bakersfield" of his and my California origins, the segment of that Earth
disintegrating, cracking before the new pumping technologies, degrading
sinister politics, sucking by the billions of gallons oil and water to fuel the

Valley agribusinesses and land boom, whole sections withered and turned to salt, grafted to the earliest background of murder and head bounty – that these references again cannot encompass.

Saturday April 3rd 2004: Heard Blue Whales can communicate in over two thousand miles of open sea – their sounds or callings so resonant at decibels below hum and hearing that the vibrations can shake a house and its windows and saw on this same day images from the California Youth Authority's prison camps for juveniles: guards beating children with unchecked brutality. Such startling jeopardies of opposition, the blinding trance of the two occurrences reminds me of Pound rising in clarity of horror over war profits, stupidity, squalor of mind and world and then sinks in equal squalor of degradations similar to Madison Grant who caged an actual "Pigmy" for weeks in the Bronx Zoo and wrote the "Passing of the Great Race," a rant which became central to the formation of Nazi ideology. Hitler in response wrote Grant a personal letter proclaiming that the book was his, Hitler's, "Bible." That "Pigmy" erupts once more in the spectre of Guantanamo and the secret prisons America has "out-sourced" on a planet-wide basis, what the horizon of "rendition" actually is and looks out over; the shoulder of this "caged" man and America seething with these previous initiations fueling Hitler's impulses and which now must include Alberto Gonzales' definitions of the "trite."

Lascivious the war's need   to   be   real
        whispers   unallowed
                    Olmec appraisals of the Nation's flesh

    serial   futures   the priests   knew

            Bursting of   cisterns
            filthy   waters

Kokolil:

The flaying

red   weir   bees

drinking the wells dry

descended is his shit
descended are his balls

Fathers of the land at the ends of their words
tied faces of the words

having been turned to blackness and still turning pulling madness

A bone that was a Year?
Who saw it?
Who knew the Word Impersonator?

One hill
of human proportion
no matter how thin
to be
clung to
7 for the deadly swimmer
number the dead
over this
and the world
begins

They walked into a canyon near King Lear Peak as it overlooks the Black Rock Desert. Some old burials were there and they wanted to remind themselves about certain things. There were eagles circling the upper sandstones and it was quiet enough so you could about hear the wind thrush the feathers of their flexed tails. That didn't last long. The noise of big engine pick-ups ripped at the Mesozoic cliffs. The two friends, a Kiowa and Shoshoni, climbed a ridge for a better look. The trucks had thrown up a contrail of dust but that didn't block what the men down below were after. A small herd of horses, fifteen or twenty boxed in. The animals trying to get a distance that would never exist again. The people in those trucks came to a stop. Got out. Reached into the open beds for chain saws. The two friends could see them fiddling with gas, oil, the spitted introductory revs of the smoking machines. It didn't take long. And you could hear the animals scream above the pitch of steel and those razors churned through Equus meat like that was no more than a salt engulfed slug. The horses stared at what was happening to them, at the men who'd do such a thing who were tossing still quivering horse sections into a pile. Those boys and their equipment had bathed and it didn't seem to the two Indians any different than what had taken place off Newfoundland and the Gulf of St. Lawrence all the open years back when walruses by the millions got brain clubbed, the sixteenth century coves from Quebec City to Cape Freels, to the nameless canyon where they now stood were forever the poised beginning come with its kiss, and whether it was Basque fisherpeople or these ranchers the hemorrhage had the same calling card and where it had drifted to they didn't know but felt those people they were watching would redesign the feast and the butcher, make it so America would maybe like the taste of itself better'n anything else.

January 28th 2004: Two stories on this same day. Pictures of the Martian landscape from the lens of "Opportunity." Place of profound strangeness – a whole "could have been" and "a could be world" of human speculation and will AND THE SOIL HERE ON EARTH. Thousands of different types. The living vast range of fertility and Life/Seed threatened by extinction – this wonderful planet and the pictures of a sterile shattered ash heap poised to become incomprehensibly the Next World in place of a Dead Earth Fate and its designs by the generation of rulers who seem in their Ahanian selves of shadowy pomp fondling the shade worlds of mournful dread and to be in conjunction with Lawrence's passage in the "Plumed Serpent":

"Kate as a woman, feared the women more than the men. The women were little and insidious, the men were bigger and more reckless. But in the eyes of each, the uncreated center, where the evil and insolence lurked.

And sometimes, she wondered whether America really was the great death-continent, the great *No!* to the European and Asiatic and even African *Yes!* Was it really the great melting pot, where men from the creative continents were smelted back again, not to a new creation, but down into the homogeneity of death? Was it the great continent of the undoing, and all its peoples the agents of the mystic destruction? Plucking, plucking at the created soul in a man, till at last it plucked out the growing germ, and left him a creature of mechanism and automatic reaction, with only one inspiration, the desire to pluck the quick out of every living spontaneous creature.

Was that the clue to America, she sometimes wondered. Was it the great death-continent, the continent that destroyed again what the other continents had built up. The continents whose spirit of place fought purely to pick the eyes out of the face of God. Was that America?

And all the people who went there, Europeans, negroes, Japanese, Chinese, all the colours and the races, were they the spent people, in whom the God impulse had collapsed, so they crossed to the great continent of the negation, where the human will declared itself "free," to pull down the soul of the world? Was it so? And did this account for the great drift to the New World, the drift of spent souls passing over to the side of Godless democracy, energetic negation? The negation which is the life-breath of materialism. And would the great negative pull of the Americans at last break the heart of the world?"

A wheeled cougar whistle   pierces   the   dead ears
of   the   dead.   The   underworld   beast   has straight legs

      flanged   at   their   ends   holes punched for   axles.

The association of ease however does not exist   and the   wheels
inspire   no   utility   no solution to burden

     The cougar's   tongue is swollen
              hangs   in   desperation
from   a   twisted   face.

      Rabies   tears   at   its   eyes   and   jaws

    and   the   wheels   are   hydrophobic   insignias

    flowing   water   and   rain

       viral   convenience
       disshaping water of   mind

    and mind/earth

There's a gap in the geologic history of Michigan called "The Lost Interval." To call it huge is to call upon an abyss that makes the nine days and nights it takes in some stories for the dead to fall into the lands where they go seem like the candle in the sunshine trying to keep up with the vast spiders and their fiery tracks as they swim across infinity. It's almost like an apology but one too infested with nothing and what's beyond nothing as it labors at its stupendous circumferences. What's lost is two-hundred-eighty-million years of geologic time from the end of the Paleozoic where the Mississippian scrunches into the Pennsylvanian to the Pleistocene. There are some microscopic plant spores from the Jurassic, whisped charmed tremblings from the Age of Dinosaurs laid down maybe in now untraceable stream valleys when Michigan was a desert and the risen land extended itself above the invading oceans and the huge Silurian reefs of the Kokomo Sea as if it were a wonderful blank where all the furies of life and death gather upon the core of dreamlessness and its petals waiting for the secret bee who never came and never will. The Iroquois did something similar in the mid-1600s. Set out on an extinction campaign against the Huron, Jesuit, Cat, Tobacco, Neutral, and Fire Nations. They made what's now known as Huronia, the old floor of Ice Age Lake Algonquin, a fertile plane extending from the southern Georgian Bay to the flats of Lake Erie, into a home sale vacuum cleaner demonstration gobbling any opposing humanity, a place they loved to visit and till its human emptiness until alcohol, cooking pots with their iron, and the lust for vengeance a hundred years later began making that wilderness from north of Albany to the Carolinas and from there to the edges of the Missouri into a version of decay where it is said in some chronicles they took to biting each other like dogs.

> Sown walnut
> keep the day
> from boring holes in our heads

bits of light make the mountains ugly this morning

deer and cliff brutal   with hanging ice

but there is   blood and lymph to be grown
                to belong to
                and already

Moon rises
with her abductions

And when the welders came to do their on-the-spot miracles his mother
fixed up tortillas with lima beans and string beef strung with Mexican
cheese. Maybe she was trying to make up for that Spanish part, the one
with its mists and ice winding her into a suspension over what her conqueror ancestors had imposed. All the long interference nailed to this bean
when those horsemen looked up 460 years ago at the montane upheavals
they'd spread from the Isles of Desolation to the rise of the Bully Choop
as it heads skyward up the Trinity River. The Andes ridges were terraced
and cultivated from sea level to nearly fifteen thousand feet. But among the
uglinesses they brought with them there was one symbolic and retributive
core out of which the other rivers of their contempt might dissolve more
completely what they'd come upon. The Inca had under cultivation close
to as many plant species as all the farmers of Europe and Asia combined.
On their hand nurtured continental spires they grew vegetables, roots,
fruit, legumes, nuts, and grains. No wheel. No iron. No animals to pull
harrow at the soils of their invention yet abundance enough for over fifteen
million added to a three-to-seven year food supply locked in storage
against the hosts of the unexpected. The suppression went down all the
way to food itself. His mother would try to get him and that sister of his

to eat such things as Mashua, a plant inhabiting two realms of beauty. Eaten raw the world of its tubers tastes of pepper, just this side of over-hot. With a good boiling though, it goes the way to sweet and is even considered in the land of its first appearances as a fine dessert. Its second realm of delicacy has to do with its close relationship to the garden nasturtium which makes it a close beauty contest rival and in the Inca, Moche, and Paracas gardens the two were more often than not grown together, the one, for its radiant, edible flowers, the other, for its frost tolerant, insect immune tuber. Or she'd plant Kiwicha. But only five or six rows in her garden. Show the Farmer there was something to compete with the fields of roses he's strung all the way to the bluffs of the Santa Ana. And this, one of the most spectacular crops on any Earth has broad leaves, stems and flowers that run purple, red, and gold with ancient fields that must have looked like the sun sets and rises of planets their trance enshrouded priestesses saw on the one or two journeys they might have taken a lifetime to train themselves for. But the Farmer wouldn't let it go beyond those few rows no matter how it attracted his sense of beauty. He knew about the Gods made out of Kiwicha's seeds saturated with dried blood on the top precipices of certain pyramids and didn't want the way beauty and delicacy turned a secret corner toward the exotic violences of his wife's ancestral enchantments and the ones of the conqueror of which she was a part also and would use the Amaranth to tell her even though he knew each plant could birth over a hundred thousand seeds and be worth the fortune his Hollywood producer boyhood friends could never hallucinate even with their movies its beauty would stop there in that garden and if she wanted to feed his children such things why go the goddamnedhead but don't forget the lox and whitefish, shove it down their throats too. And it's not that the food of others hasn't been rejected, been found tasteless or worse, a half nausea to be best left alone or left to the peoples who like it for their reasons but that the conqueror even suppressed the growing and ordered the discoveries of thousands of years to be ended. Plants with the names of Tarwi, Lucuma, Oca have lain upon the unwhispered high slopes of these regions for nearly five hundred years with no curious palate to receive their taste, the shrinkage even sterility waiting for the rescue his mother figured would never arrive even if him and that sister carried those ingredients in their grammar school lunch boxes for the next thousand years.

Read of an extraordinary find January 2004 in Germany: a recently discovered cave with Paleolithic artifacts – mammoth ivory figurines of astonishing delicacy. A horse's head, a mallard in graceful glide with folded wings as if ready to begin its descent toward a pond, a lion-like shrouded man-figure. The works are supremely skillful and may date to 35,000BP. The horse has its ears folded back, its head arched as if ready for combat against a rival. Or flight, or, if a mare, then in the pose of suckling a new-born colt. On the same day of this reported Paleolithic find a fabrication was revealed. Nazi "werewolves" carried on a campaign of sabotage in the post-occupation months after the Second World War. Their depredations were compared to the insurgency in Iraq by C. Rice and D. Rumsfeld except no casualties were ever recorded due to these "werewolf incidents." The fabrication can be traced to a Rupert Murdoch front man from "Fox News" – Rand Simberg by name, described as a consultant in "space commercialization," "space tourism," and "Internet Security." These slippery new solar system identities at the heart of the Bush proposal for a first post-Rapture "Moon Colony" for which Iraq is essential as stepping stone to Mars; the raw materials necessary to produce the time for such technological development for the new electro-ion rockets and their extra-terrestrial launch pads.

Curate the service and ceremony. Chomp at the little ponds of violence that brush the nostrils with their ghost petaled ripples attracting only the most impassive funerals and mutilations in every one of their sultry immensities. "Cockulating" – the cowboy name for it. One thing maybe to go cock-hungry. Pleasure however unreliable its appearances may still be considered good luck, occasion for even the deepest laughter over how funny and mortal people can really let themselves get. He'd even worked among the Mormons once after leaving Oklahoma. Stayed awhile doing ranch labors in Nevada riding fences and one day up ridge saw what he thought was a stray cow clicked his cutting horse pulled his lasso proceeded to ride up quiet so as not to over surprise the animal and its lover the ranch owner was being a kind of grim reaper there one never yet ever seen but it'd be better to get out of ear shot before hearing any other kind of news those Great Basin Wastes produced. Maybe it's radiation that done it. The Atomic Energy Commission scared to say it'd killed just about everyone everything except some select Americans who in the depths of their sickness would take out to chase their wildest gone to the wild cows. What with the fact there were whorehouses that they were legal with actual human ladies in them might never have occurred. Yup. Probably. "Finders fuckin Keepers" he thought. Maybe none of 'em ever was pretty as that cow. She had a nice hide. Yet he rode back anyways, properly fed, watered, brushed down his horse, packed up his stuff and started walking to California or Venus; anywhere a Ghost Dance would set'im down was fine, get to some fringe, run out into another piece of hanging spit was all he wanted to ask the narrations about what the world would look like after the men and women of this one rubbed themselves invisible finally.

In early March of 2004 we set out on a thousand mile expedition to Scammon's Lagoon at Guerro Negro, Baja, California. The outfitter; a surfer and trail guide from Ensenada who got his masters degree in eco-tourism, knows the wildernesses and the dangerous lures of their mysteries. The journey traversed landscapes of flora unlike anything we'd ever seen along with mountains and plains which still lie unexplored in the far distances.

We drove through forests of cardons (relative of the sajuaro), giants living 500 to 600 years spectacularly formed with twisted arms and trunks, cirios (related to the ocotillo) with their strange sinuous bodies and leaf forms that look like galatic clusters. Elephant trees and "patallios" or tree yuccas along with blooming coastal agave and startling outcrops of verbena. These landscapes are almost waterless and there are mountain sheep evolved in their wilds that never drink water yet in the late afternoon of our first traveling day we experienced a rare desert cloud burst and four spectacular rainbows (one a triple and another, a quadruple) that seemed to beckon our van over a fifteen mile period as we crossed the 28th parallel from Northern Baja to Southern Baja and began an adventure unlike anything we could have ever imagined.

At 6:00am on the following morning we set out on Scammon's Lagoon in a kind of light outboard driven dory. The body of water is named for the whale ship captain who invaded this aquatic nursery in the nineteenth century for the grey whales which still come here to birth their calves and prepare the newborn for the trials of the open sea where killer whales wait along with white shark for any sign of the vulnerable. It is a haven where mothers, nurses, and the newborn attend to each other and form lifelong bonds. Scammon discovered the nursery and hunted and killed and the cows in their fury responding with equal violence were named "Devil Fish" by the whalers for the way the crew members were crushed and ripped to pieces by the slashing bodies of these cetaceans who protected their young. I kept thinking of the passages from Melville's episode in "Moby Dick," "The Grand Armada" where the crew of the Pequod, after outrunning pirates in the Sunda Straits came upon the strangest lake of being ever recorded; fiction or non-fiction for me it has made a lasting difference as both an act of imagination and the depiction of a blinding scale of quiet and cold murder.

The Lagoon this morning was unusually calm. We could see dolphin and sea lion off our bow, huge osprey and pelican flying over us and a magnificent coastal desert with mountain ranges in the distances which hold in their secret arroyos and oasis ancient cave art. The Crespi Expedition came through here 250 years ago and I think this is what San Diego or

San Francisco may have looked like as those initial encounters began moving toward the ceaseless boilings of the following centuries. There was also a huge flock of birds we could not identify appearing and disappearing in their unison of flexed bodies having the rhythms of a ghostly Maya fan moving across the vanishing point of water and sky at the farthest horizon.

The guide began to slow and in this silence the backs and sides of grey whales surfaced all around us, cows and calves arching up, exposing their spines and flukes; glittering, and slithering into the depths, great mammalian dragons, their spouts creating instant flower-like rainbows over the nearly glass-like water nursery. We could hear the huge animal breathings, the wind carrying their breath-spray and ourselves immersed in the raptures of these life sounds for maybe an hour, maybe more as we waited, drifted, and listened.

A single cow suddenly rose up from the whale generated sea-whip. At first she appeared and then subsided; ascended again and then let us touch her. She was 45 feet long and had extraordinary control of her tremendous body. She could float on her back under our small boat not moving even an inch for minutes as she watched us with her great eye or turned and floated up to the side of the dory, her fifteen foot barnacle-scarred head fully exposed, her blow hole expanding in spray with the force of geyser, her breath really like a small volcano and she let us touch her in those remarkable minutes. We could see her flukes, her huge fins, her multicolored body as she floated around us in circles, gentle, curious, elegant, distinct and I don't know quite how to reach for any of the words that might help me to say how suddenly relieved we were of cynicism and malice and the human accumulation as this whale after nearly two hours turned in her last circumambulations and quietly, almost lightly vanished.

That afternoon we searched tide pools and the remains of huge piers, wind and sea-eaten things let loose and dilated in the destroyings. Under stone we found octopus, sea stars and steel girders lay everywhere in sharp, grotesque disintegration.

Following morning up early again then out to the same Lagoon area as the day before but the whales off, aloof, gliding away from us, their tremendous backs a-sheen with sunlight, gorgeous, cascading water. Asking what other instances there could possibly be after our previous encounter we went ashore for lunch, some talk, a walk through the streets of Guerro Negro, a colony owned and run by Mitsubishi with its private neighborhood of managers and workers; a salt mine; basically a salt leeching process producing millions of tons of sea salt. Cured and dried in the fierce sun, workers in uniform coming and going from various shifts and behemoth salt trucks the size of ocean going barges driven at these edges with eighteen foot high tires. A nearly billion dollar industry relentlessly seething at the boundaries of this lagoon where the whales have come for a million, two million, or 700,000 years? No one knows. The "eco-tourism" good for publicity and the UN mandate that this geography be designated a world treasure with its flora and fauna and wild emptinesses dribbling into the unfolding immensities the salt trucks at these shores appear to be testing as equipment for ore extraction here and on asteroids carrying their 250 ton loads to cargo ships waiting at new piers and depots ready for construction and the whales and their story and their lagoon fastened to these other certainties and detachments and asteroidal vagueries, premonitions, methane seas waiting for what corporate yachts?

2:00 pm. Another larger dory outfitted at Marizial. The Lagoon more unstable, wind and choppy sea. Huge whale heads appearing in the distances

and to our sides:
huge bodies
the rising and falling of these
seem almost
disappearances from previous
game." Our guide wants to
but what we see
and marvelous and enough
to shut down the engine

one here, one there, or breaching their
in hills of sea spray and sea play
giant heads makes the sea surface
like a game board of appearances and
creations gathered here for a "guessing
tryfor an episode like yesterday's
seems so elfish and rare
we say but the guide decides
and drift none of us expecting in the

standstill or knowing
no whales, only wind and sea-
when just at the moment
a whale and her calf appeared
thin craft the mother nudging
touch this child and for an hour
with their fins
showered us
and examined us
we they
in these permissions and
the intimacy the strange
bewilderment
rising as an uneasy phantasm
or realize before this moment
an inviolable penetration of
remote cripplings
of skilled totalitarianisms
disciplined future of earth-
as species preparation
and technology a
properly managed slaveries
years?

what to expect so we drifted;
chop 40 minutes of it
of re-kindling the engine for shore
on the side of what seemed our paper-
her recently born infant letting us
they played with us pressed our boat
gently watched and looked
 in their breath spray floated under
as thoroughly
and as startlingly as they appeared
curiosities they dissolved
communion the elaborate tender
and incomprehensible gentleness
no knowing can properly hold
of what was it trust between species
being gently relieving the terrible
humanity has embraced the siege
that will be necessary for the
abandonment for what will it take
the array of propaganda
chronology of control and
for 2000 to 3000

As we came ashore the coastal desert wetlands seemed to fill with sandpiper, large osprey floating above nests and nestlings, white heron, peregrine falcon searching for ripe meat well hidden in the barely penetrable labyrinths of scrub by the other bird species, and shadowy deer and coyote lurking warily listening and smelling at the fringes. I have never experienced a creaturely encounter such as this (if that is what it was) no matter how commercialized its context as "eco-tourism" might finally be and Melville's passages quicken mirrors of perplexity that remain intensely inaccessible and secretive:

" . . . we glided between two whales into the innermost heart of
shoal, as if from some mountain torrent we had slid into a serene
lake. Here the storms in the roaring glens between the outermost
whales, were heard but not felt. In this central expanse the sea presented that smooth, satin-like surface, called a sleek produced by
the subtle moisture thrown off by the whale in his more quiet
moods . . . Keeping at the center of the lake, we were occasionally
visited by small tame cows and calves; the women and children of
this routed host . . ."

The whalers were killing at the margins of this "lake" and Melville both
astonished and shamed by the human business mentions

" . . . this circumstance, because, as if the cows and calves had been
purposefully locked up in this innermost fold; and as if the wide
extent of the herd had hitherto prevented them from learning the
precise cause of its stopping or, possibly being so young unsophis-
ticated and everyway innocent and inexperienced, however it may
have been, these smaller whales – now and then visiting our
becalmed boat from the margin of the lake – evinced a wondrous
fearlessness and confidence, or else a still becharmed panic which
it was impossible not to marvel at. Like house-hold dogs they came
sniffing round us, right up to our gunwales, and touching them.
Queequeg patted their foreheads; Starbuck scratched their backs
with his lance; but fearful of the consequences, for the time refrained
from darting it. But far beneath the wondrous world upon the
surface, another and still stranger world met our eyes as we gazed
over the side. For, suspended in those watery vaults, floated the forms
of the nursing mothers of the whales, and those that by their enormous girth seemed shortly to become mothers. The lake, as I have
hinted, was to a considerable depth exceedingly transparent, and as

human infants while suckling will calmly and fixedly gaze away from the breast, as if leading two different lives at the same time; and while yet drawing mortal nourishment, be still spiritually feasting upon some unearthly reminiscence; – even so did the young of these whales seem looking up toward us, but not at us, as if we were but a bit of Gulf weed in the newborn sight. Floating on their sides, the mothers also seemed quietly eyeing us. One of these little infants, that from certain queer tokens seemed hardly a day old, might have measured some four- teen feet in length, and some six feet in girth. He was a little frisky though as yet his body seemed scarce yet recovered from that irksome position it had so lately occupied in the maternal reticule; where tail to head, and all ready for the final spring, the unborn whale lies bent like a Tartar's bow. The delicate side-fins, and the palms of his flukes, still freshly retained the plaited crumple appearance of a baby's ears newly arrived from foreign parts . . ."

And, so not to mistake the exact presence of the crew and its labors, this footnote regarding the fertile cows:

" . . . a contingency provided for in suckling by two teats, curiously situated, one on each side of the anus; but the breasts themselves extend upwards from that. When by chance these precious parts in a nursing whale are cut by the hunter's lance, the mother's pouring milk and blood rivalingly discolor the sea for rods. The milk is very sweet and rich; it has been tasted by man; it might do well with strawberries . . ."

The "it might do well with strawberries" might mix with the chronicles of first contact between the French and numerous tribes of the Great Lakes at the beginning of the seventeenth century. Those inland fresh water seas and their adjacent forests became a house of slaughter ("Toes are scarce among veteran blubber room men") slippery with blood and gore as any "Pequod." The peltry in beaver served with lead-laced brandy offered a number of the smaller tribes an invitation to extinction more potent than even their ancient vision quests. Those hunts as Melville knew them too, surfacing as a repository rimming his about-to-be-coldly-treasured futures as he stirred up the malignancies, the wonders, grievances, and the terrible fineness of his, to use Lawrence's still watchfully clear adjective, "unearthly" swarms of enormities hovering over the vessel of Democracy. The sea of oils and blood finally becoming the mutated hydrocephaly of modern empire as Melville's great grandson, Paul Metcalf in his "Genoa" seems to have recognized, setting the human brain afloat in the wandering charts of Columbus onward.

Thick oil's
color of cream
lures neighbors
come to lick or chew
the units of currency made standard:

One winter prime adult beaver equaled
10 lbs. feathers
8 moose hoofs
a brass kettle or
one and half pounds gunpowder

The Huron women loved this bribery and its speculation. But the commerce could not make even their dead safe from such sweet nausea based upon a phonetics whose irritation fed monopoly; the upper country ". . . from the foot up inside of each hind leg to the anal vent and from there up the belly and breast to the middle of the lower lip, and from each forepaw up the inside of the leg to the center slit at the chest . . ."

When it was another world there were piles of fine ambergris. Sperm, bowhead, and fin whales found their way up the ancient rivers; the Hudson Channel via the Mohawk and earlier drainages of Lake Ontario, or the initial scourings of the St. Lawrence. There were herds of walrus and if any of those great things died they'd lay on shore to be sniffed by woodland musk ox, a long-legged taller than a buffalo first arriver who apparently loved the edge of the retreating ice or the walrus could wait till the sixteenth century when they'd get brain clubbed by the millions. The climate was cold, wet, perfect for the spruce groves that came to the border of those seas and rivers, the Mississippi and Illinois with whales breaching at their surfaces. There were peccaries too, and woodland caribou, bison, the huge moose-like Cervalces that siphoned lake bottom. The mysterious giant beaver weighed in at over four hundred eighty pounds, almost big as a black bear, and a superb swimmer. Yet its incisors compared with its modern sixty pound relative seem much weaker in their jaw attachments, those teeth ending in blunted tips. Tall tales from the highest Eskimo barrens south tell about beaver dams so vast whole ice smothered valleys got drowned, that nothing could stop the six inch gnawers, that everything then was gigantic and the beaver supplied all the mud from which the mountains were made, and waterfalls, and caves. Right to the eighteenth century the Chippewa told about the Castoroides swimming the small rivers of their country still. That ancient air also offered its oxygen to the Mastodon and Jefferson Mammoth. Both elephants were just about everywhere in the Ice Age forests. The mastodon liked the browse, spruce twigs and leaves were perfect for the blunt cusps of their teeth that worked up and down on the hard fodder of their preference. The mammoth were grazers with teeth that slid forward and backward. When the ice retreated depressions were left on the land, kettle holes that filled with silt and clay, aquatic vegetation, the live and the dead. When the kettles eventually became bogs they also became luring quaking traps with an apparently solid surface. Those proboscideans stepped there, stepped out for a last feast, particularly in winter when everything to be sensed was froze. They crashed through shoulder high, in long enough to know and sink before the disappointed eyes of the human and non-human neighborhood flesh masters.

There's a mastodon drowned approximately 14,000 years ago re-upped for appearances in the late nineteenth century as a bog corpse, one of the oldest citizens of Cohoes New York, sucked at the earliest waters of the Hudson River with that prehensile trunk and now lies in the New York State Museum at Albany.

Got a tour one day in the late twentieth century, a curator walked Gail and me through storage corridors and bins and on one table there rested the skull and vertebra of this North American elephant. Got to hold it, touch it, feel its teeth, rub its massive forehead and the waves and indentations of bone which held the muscle masses, nerves, and sinew of its trunk. Say it weighed more than Ginsberg's "hydrogen jukebox" on a hot desert afternoon at about ten-to-ten on the Doomsday Clock, that wristwatch of sorrows someone kept setting once upon a time but seems to have just been placed in a forgotten drawer. The Cahoes Mastodon also reminded me of my play on the shore line of the La Brea Tar Pits when I was a boy. The petroleum welling up, split, the bubble membranes at the surface stunk like the discarded crank cases of my father's tractors stuck in a grease pit. Mastodon and mammoth were at that shoreline too, giant camel, ground sloth of various orders, short faced bear, saber toothed tigers, and huge American lions looking to stave off starvation in their twelve to fourteen hundred pound bodies. The hungry at La Brea and in those glacial kettles either broke their teeth or throats on what was wandering the walls of that motel with their off-trailer assemblies.

The Being that is Faceless some of the forest tribes called Death. The flesh and brain-body wandering, to become immune to Earth. Everything on it thick with blind darkness, And only words can bring the mind back. The Three Rare Words: EAR THROAT EYE. To remind the living the sun rises and sets. The sky is wonderful. That no one can be indifferent to the work of life. True indifference is reserved for insanity and the Day the Earth Splits.

I'd hear my mother's stories looking at maps of dream canyons and deserts, plains and mountains balanced on nothing more than some sum of evaporations she distantly referred to and the mysteries of wordlessness from her receding world out of which ceremonials, dance, and writing pictures were made. She loved how language was poised there. And that human breath was one, a fine choice for sight and sound and mind and what words might hold in their unreachable cores. But that was one only. And so a person by earliest guidance in those traditions could choose. Yet who could tell in any life of leftovers about the unraveled secrets that have been made into carnivals where tourists crowd, to gawk and buy the desperate attempts to say that there even was a world where war and hunting all those centuries up to the nineteenth killed most, from there to alcohol and a jail cell, one that didn't do that dance of meiosis or mitosis, but just stays the same and grinds the living into the dead. My mother could hear the names of earlier men: "Making Medicine, the Faithful" "White Goose" or plain "Teeth" the raider who loved the beautiful horses in Mexico. What happened to males when all their flesh got piled, the forbidden revelation tapping at the heart with its wonder and fatigue over the mountain time can become stuffing you down its enormous throat, and her own relatives who also got shut away in Missions or became the quarry of an "Indian Shoot." I'd think about my mother and what it meant personally to kill a California grizzly. One of my first memories is of her trying to tell me about her mother and grandmothers; who she was extending back to the

Crespi Expedition and farther into the Aztec roots of Mexico. Her proportions were still of the nineteenth century and perhaps even earlier backward spills; 4'10" with small thin hands, wore her very black thick hair in various buns with elaborate combs she inherited and when she let it fall the folds extended to below her knees. Her mother was last of a line of "Californios" horse women from Santa Cruz, the Salinas Valley, and the Sierra foothills families who owned vast tracks of land and intermarried with the Indians, wandering lumber jacks, and banditos taken to murder in their rage over the murdering gringos. When she felt her explanation could go no further she read to me and my sister from "Up and Down California in 1860-1864" the Journal of William H. Brewer, as distinct an adventure in its smaller way as the Journey of Lewis and Clarke:

> "We spent the next day there looking up the adjacent hills. The road for the first three days from Santa Barbara was more traveled than any we had seen before. The first 'Overland' through Santa Barbara, on Monday evening, April 1, was celebrated with the firing of cannon, etc. Many emigrants were passing over the road. One long train was bound for Texas, sick of California. One meets many such uneasy families who have lived in Ohio or Michigan, then Kansas or Iowa, then California or Oregon, and now for Texas or somewhere else.

And among those so early and already disappointed and broken hosts who have come to California appeared another wholly separate group:

> "Several small companies of five to ten passed us on horseback, native (Spanish Californian), traveling for pleasure or business, on horseback with one or two pack-mules along with baggage. The women wear black hats with feathers, much like a Kossuth hat, ordinary (not long 'riding') dresses, often of gay colors. They ride with

feet on the 'right' side of the horse, sitting nearly squarely crosswise, both feet hanging down as if they are sitting on a bench. Often a strap ornamented with silver and tassels, or a mere red sash, is tied over lap, holding them firmly in the saddle. No horse can throw them; they would go sweeping past us at a California gallop. We came on two or three parties at their noon lunch. They will ride sixty or seventy miles in a day and not complain . . ."

And,

"I wish you could see those Mexican ladies ride; you would say you never saw riding before. Our American girls along could not shine at all. There seems to be a peculiar talent in the Spanish race for horsemanship; all ride gracefully, but I never saw ladies in the East who could approach the poorest of the Spanish ladies whom I have yet seen ride. I cannot well convey an adequate conception of the way they went galloping over the fields-squirrel holes. ditches, and logs are no cause of stopping-jumping a fence or a gulch if one was in the way . . ."

My mother and her people had remnants still far into the twentieth century; saddles, various leather gear with silver trappings, and a box full of feathers similarly referred to here – osprey, golden eagle, roadrunner, egret, condor, every one faded into the sorrows along with a fox jaw, some large rattles of what must have been a huge rattlesnake, and grizzly teeth. Why these items? I wouldn't have known how to approach apparently such simple question due to my mother's moods whenever this box made its sly, almost wearisome appearances. There were references to death associated with what I thought as a child were the three most unconsoling and yet queerest items among that haunted containment that strikes to this day with the same chills that mocked me as a boy. The fox took the life of an infant girl with its rabid bite in the 1840s, the rattler bit one of my great earlier aunts and who died in agony of gangrenous suffocation; the grizzly killed the favorite horse of one of my 1820s grandfathers, a grizzly hunting horse he'd precisely trained for its courage and intelligence, and was furious over the death, tracked down the bear himself, extracted these teeth and left the animal to rot after pissing on its eyes.

There are also references to space as it was comprehended at that time; vistas from coastal foothills where the surveyors could see for three or four hundred miles and moments of quiet curiosity and unembarrassed wonder:

"On passing the Santa Lucia the entire aspect of the country changed. It was as if we had passed into another land and another clime. The Salinas Valley thus far is much less verdant than we anticipated. There are more trees but less grass. Imagine a plain ten to twenty miles wide, cut up by valleys into innumerable hills from two to four hundred feet high, their summits of nearly the same level. Their sides rounded into gentle slopes. The soil is already dried and parched, the grass already dry as hay, except along the streams, the hills brown as a stubble field. But scattered over these hills and in these valleys are trees every few rods – great oaks, often of immense size, ten, twelve, eighteen and more feet in circumference, but not high; their wide-spreading branches making heads often over a hundred feet in diameter – of the deepest green foliage – while from every branch hangs a trailing lichen, often several feet long and delicate as lace. In passing over country, every hill and valley presents   a new view of these trees – here a park, there a vista with blue mountains ahead. I could never tire of watching some of these beautiful places of natural scenery. A few pines were seen for several miles, with a very open, airy habit, entirely unlike any pine I have ever seen before, even lighter and airier than the Italian pines common in Southern France by the Mediterranean. They cast but little shade . . ."

The writing is watchful, restlessly aware, lets itself wander into the fresh knowledge and saving wonders that don't want to and can't stand still before this adventure. It is also a special kind of so far little recognized work emerging from this time that wants not to be blinded by the blinding forces which impinge upon it and give it a helpless parched grandeur often, because of the prose itself written by this young geologist/geographer, who similarly to a Cabeza de Vaca or Peter Matthiessen feels deeply and uneasily the pulses he breaths before the mutilation, magnificence, and upheaval it witnesses. The passages about mining, the already leftover world mining's results impose, offer an unusual direct eye:

"All the way from Shasta here is a placer region – a high table land, furrowed into innumerable canyons and gulches. The soil is often a hundred feet thick – a very compact, red, cement gravel. In this is gold, especially in the gulches or ravines. Here in an early day miners 'picked-in' – many made their 'pile' and left, others died. Little mining towns sprang up, but as the richest placers were worked out they became deserted . . . the scenery here is unlike as can be any- thing that we have passed through before. It is a dry, hilly country, with high mountains along the north, the soil very dry and covered with scattered trees and bushes. There are gardens, etc., in the valleys, but generally the land is barren from draught. The whole region is scarred by miners, who have skimmed over the surface and left the region more desolate than before . . . Water is supplied during the summer by ditches, dug for miles in length, by which the mountain streams are carried over the lower hills and the water used for mining the dirt. When these ditches cross the gullies, the water is carried in a wooden trough, or as we in the East would say, a 'race,' but here they are universally called 'flumes.' We passed one of these flumes yesterday that ran across the valley for a distance of over five thousand feet, most the way over fifty feet high and in places over ninety feet . . ."

This passage offers some degree of scale but the references to hydraulic mining, the immediate witness carried in the diction and held in the close work of the writing without pretension gathers a ground which drifts toward us in the twenty first century full and heavy with what took place:

"The amount of soil removed in hydraulic mining must be seen to be at all appreciated. Single claims will estimate it by the millions of tons, the 'tailings' . . . fill the valleys, while the mud not only muddies the Sacramento River for more than four hundred miles of its course, but is slowly and surely filling up the Bay of San Francisco. In the Sierra the soil from hundreds of acres together has already been sluiced off from rock, which it formerly covered even to depths of 150 feet! I have seen none of the heavy mining as yet, although I have seen works and effects that one would imagine it would take centuries to produce instead of the dozen years that have elapsed since the work began . . ."

And groups of Indians haunting the world disappearing and the world to come at margins even here described which cast their chill; this author and naturalist full of good will, a strong eye for the tragic birth rites of modern California, and the claustrophobic racism which infects him. But he is nonetheless, wary and suspicious of the too easily reached for pitilessness Manifest Destiny offers, hating slavery as he does, and the already cruel and barbaric politics of the State he is exploring:

"Quite a number of Indians, 'Diggers,' were about – they often stopped near camp and stared wonderingly at us. Sometimes there would be a group of five or six in a trail that ran within a rod of our tent – their men, with their bows and arrows and long hair. The women, with their faces horribly tattooed and their heavy, thick, and coarse black hair cut off square, just even with their eyes in front but hanging down over the sides of the face and back of the head to the neck. Sometimes the women had burdens, a bundle or basket on the back carried by a strap across the forehead; sometimes they came with children, which were often entirely naked. Such groups would stop, just at evening while we were talking and smoking, and stand within a rod of us for sometime, looking intently at us, then pass us with very few words among themselves. Sometimes during the day, two or three sqaws would come along, sit down in the hot sun within three or four rods of the tent, say nothing, but listlessly watch us for half an hour together..."

What can one try to reconstruct from these descriptions? The utterly helpless sense of the alien and its invasion; these women and children at such margins as then still existed, taking a moment to study the extinguishing visitors in their twilight repose, already knowing the inescapably fatal story. Their standing. Their watching. Both sides hallowed by the paralysis, the putrescent abyss? My mother in reading such references seemed to bear the passages like a personal scar as she thought too of the Texans, Mainers, Ohioans, Pennsylvanians, Wisconsiners, Kansans, and Others to be wracked by the taunting, blinding disappointments in waiting in California which have absorbed countless hordes. And this passage which seemed so familiar to her, as if what she'd been told by her great aunts about the world before the gringo invasions were true:

"Birds scream in the air – gulls, pelicans, birds large and birds small, in flocks like clouds. Seals and sea lions bask on the rock islands close to the shore; their voices can be heard night and day. Buzzards strive for offal on the beach, crows and ravens 'caw' from the trees, while hawks, eagles, owls, vultures, etc., abound. These last are enormous birds, like a condor, and nearly as large. We have seen some that would probably weigh fifty or sixty pounds, and I have frequently picked up their quills over two feet long- one thirty inches – and I have seen them thirty-two inches long. They are called condors by the Americans. A whale was stranded on the beach, and tracks of grizzlies were thick about it . . ."

I can remember still, in my childhood, my mother calling the family out to watch a sunset sky for the huge birds as they flew over the rose fields.

It seemed that city had let up some curtain and pulled me into another world. I'd spend whole afternoons listening to stories about the Mississippi Delta, the mixture of poor Black and poor White. Families picked up with nothing, to go north, finally by the millions to get to factories smoking just beyond the edges of human noise made by the liquor and hot bodies come for another kind of ride, not necessarily relief, because they'd have to wear a mask again, but there they could smile, ease up, even let a white boy come close without killing him. Pool made part of it possible. The other half was I could dance. Looked good doing it, and knew. My sister taught me the introductory moves. The lure a body can be telling the strangest stories about desire and the just as sudden death of desire spilling into the secret reaches of the fingertips and eyelids and how before every dance she'd set her hair. And the razors. Set those with extra squirts of "Spray Net" in the halo of the bouffant. Set the blackness of her eyes in pencil. Joke over boyfriends headed to jail after throwing their arms dead as major league rookies. Fuck hard enough. Fuck herself out of them into another place beyond the car wrecks and knife fights of her night rides from

Escondido to Cucamonga. And my mother. Her stories about the Anahuac. Her Aztec susceptibilities coming forward in the whispered desert nights while our family's roses, closed in their petals, waited for the sun to spread them, delicate leafage heavy, swelling with penetration of the hot initial waves of light showing themselves over the cracked pendants of the recently born mountains suspended and withheld in the distance. She'd start with flutes. Telling anyone who'd hear about the holes in that clay. Each flute carrying four, and producing a five tone scale for intensity and eroticism. She'd do this after too much mescal, after eating the worm. Talk about the Auanime, the Aztec Majas who accompanied the warrior businessmen and their scratching dances, ticklish provocation before the men, the city, the gods who needed dancing, called for it with every pattern a body could make in the air. People wanting and sleepless. The flowered body and flowered word rising in them toward the legendary shrine with its inner walls of gold and emerald and jade intersperced with woven feathers where they could adore the Uncreated and go to the House of Dwarfs filled with rabbits, those trembling ears ready to gush with night flower scents of murder. My mother took me to see the Arapaho and Hopi ceremonials, told me about the Indians and patterns made by the head, the movements of the arms and feet. Out of the pageantry they could summon hunchbacks and dwarfs acrobats and frenzies make the obsidian of their knives into sepulchers and compulsions of messiah perfumes or just go home little fucker and pour ice on your balls.

Slowly he found they carried knives too, quiet and steady and real. Not for show. But in range. To be drawn and used. You could concentrate both ways on that mirror. Let the veil of race go. I knew they had shown me the sexual garments of the degradation. Sex mummy come to bathe everyone in something huger than any Egypt ever was or could be. It scared me how they let me sway before them, let their drops of permission sweetly splash, and watched, knowing this boy in his whiteness. What I had come to ask, and maybe, for them, what they became ready to give.

Death run on an empty belly can't get away from the suicide
masters   water lily   cool   our   bodies
longing to be murdered by the   nearest   feather

In the murals there are battles for human bodies. The love of torture part of the nourishment. A snack for the alert starving Gods the fathers will mutilate their tongues for to satisfy the birth of new rule in the sons who would be the risen kings in their service to neuter the language leave hole in smallest utterance for Anthrax Politics lesions on the pre-breath formations of our words flooding the first houses with sand wasps nests tailings of the story's gamble.

She blushed and for a second hoped the coloration might dam the faraway sounds of words. The breath of the hanging syllables began to beat rawly. She could let them grow there, into a judgement. She let them throb instead into faintnesses, let them slightly embarrass her and her memories of bodies and lovers whose transitions and defiances may be the only living reassurances she'd ever really known. "Promises" the ones she knew could end in lost jobs, prison, broken houses, or being stalked by the police. There were other endings too but she couldn't let them form, more as a courtesy to dam memories because some of the men and women she'd known had had to live those ends and which rendered her suspect before her own world, the one draped as the edifice of an invisible longing before the catastrophies of loneliness and self loathing.

get a bath   come clean take on the friendliest colors
of your surroundings though the mind casts
on   daily   killings   the self   persuasions   sweeping that   region
like   they   were   meat   birds   with   no   names   yet
assigned   to   them   but   tinged   still   in last   breath

signaling to air   dry   grasses   trembling   with   how   close
the   thousand   eared   night   comes

to   voices   leaning   on   the   half   eaten   rains
and   nothing   spared

Robert Duncan in considering Robert Browning, colonialism, war, and
the empire of the modern war state (that Blake knew did and would
impinge on "everything that lives") wrote: "These poems where many
persons from many times and places begin to appear-as in the 'Cantos,'
'The Waste Land,' 'Finnegan's Wake,' 'The War Trilogy,' and 'Paterson,'
– are poems of a world mind in process. The seemingly triumphant reality
of the War and State disorient the poet who is partisan to a free and
world-wide possibility, so that his creative task becomes the more imper-
ative. The challenge increases the insistence of the imagination to renew
the reality of its own. It is not insignificant that these 'poems containing
history' are all products of a movement in literature that was identified in
the beginning as free-verse..." DISORIENT. How is the poet using that
transitive verb with its seventeenth century French origins, the background of the Coeur du Bois searching the North American forests and
tundra for the "Northern Passage" to the Orient gone lost in winter ice
jungles full of disorientations; that colonialism and its enterprises including the various Indian tribes, both worlds lured into helpless fatalities
and mutual fascinations. The simplest definitions are 1. to cause to lose

bearings, 2. To displace from normal position or relationship, and the third most accurate possibility when considering the cast of the new verb over the mystery of a continent – "to cause to lose a sense of time, place, or identity"; persons both known and having been lost swallowed by those worlds. The poet adds to this verb a sense of urgency and threat. The usage of the one word recalls the terrifying questions D.H. Lawrence asks in the "Plumed Serpent" about America: is it the "great continent of the undoing" and its massed "last first people" (as Olson called us) the "agents of mystic destruction . . . pulling down the soul of the world . . ." And can the poet, individually, before what Lawrence identified as the "drift" (as if the "pulling" too is a geologic force), hold any longer the presence of a mind uncontaminated by the nullity and collapse which beckons to it. The constant subtle depletions, the purity of what Blake called "soft delusive" carelessness, enrobed and masquerading as beauty, longing, and Imagination. MindCare blunted and transformed into an intricate repellence and suffocation which slowly mutilates recognition and the desire to keep both recognition and inspiration alive in mind and heart. Such triumph, to use Duncan's term places the poet into a dread and desolation, unspeakable and hard. It reminds me of Los's Anvil in "Jerusalem" where Blake conceived of the Poet/Bard in a "Time of Trouble" releasing her or himself into the raw dangerous labors of inspiration which are often terrible, deadly, and poisonous but primordially necessary for the ancient practices of rectitude and resistance. And Blake knew his word; the archaic origins of "Trouble" lie in the skilled Roman/ Mediterranean usages of torture, oppression, and slavery. Old "Trouble" Blake saw rising in its Newtonian materialist/industrial dimensions. Where in these worships of falsehood and " . . . ghastly torment sick hanging upon the wind" as Blake calls it up in his last prophecy "The Four Zoas" lies either the poet's or anyone's mind? Duncan transforms these questions into the courage of new/ancient "creative task" to call the Imagination to its risks and works and not transform the lethal disappointments always seeking their dominion in ourselves into luring and alluring clever slumbers ("Delicious Viands" as Blake said, " . . . budding and blossoming . . ."

Last night, Thursday March 8th 2004, went to hear Martin Peterson, the Deputy Director of the CIA, a shade among interchangeable shades who talked of "American Interests, Utility and Standards." "Espionage." He defined the practice as "a long hard business." The adjectives "long" and "hard" have the carriage of their phallic simplicities. That a spokesperson of this high rank would use these parts of speech with such stark and reckless vulgarity in a public forum without the vaguest sense of their pornographic implications only three months prior to the appearances of the Abu Ghraib images marks this "business" as a General Motors Hotel Feature, Grateful Grandma Combo, Privateertainment, or XXX Training Academy with feel flesh features far or near Rita Tammy Shanghai Suzy Unbelievable Hurtdoms touchtoned engraved on the EAVESDROPLINE. SPY was never mentioned either as word or act – the secret watcher whose purpose is hostility, or the agent whose pretenses are false, clandestine, and belligerent.

Mr. Peterson gave a list of those things that cannot be done:

A. "Predict the future."

B. "Determine policy. This is up to elected officials."

C. "Remove all risks."

Does the practitioner of Darkness attempt to influence the future?

Does the practitioner of moral immoralities assume an information unimpeded by personal ideology?

Does the practitioner of murder, blackmail, torture – does one who breaks the laws of other countries and in that becomes a lawless self in the name of Democracy/America remove/rendition either individuals or societies that prove to be inconvenient?

In the pursuit of "prudent risk management" "we do not fit policy to fashion" "we do not coerce; we do not blackmail" and "law enforcement linkages" are "simply the price of poker."

In reference to weapons of mass destruction Peterson commented, "We didn't hit a home run on that one," revealing the high snobbery of the educated hand picked murderer who kills for ideals.

"Comfort" was his central word. "Comfort Zones" and the authority of Comfort scratching as some rabid jaguar at the bottom of either Hopewellian or earlier Adena Cones as those central continent ancient ravings impinge under blood or under lung?

I don't know of another word, as I recall both Robert Duncan's vocabulary and the snarled cesswells of speech delivered by Martin Peterson in the spring of 2004, the spring of Abu Ghraib, that measures as accurately the neurological symptoms of this time that have been set in motion and which, in part, defines the creature feeling, the membranous currents of trance we seem to be living in transforming knowledge, world, and courage into bone-dry frailties whose ends we cannot see or anticipate.

        Water Mountain

                progenitor of Cities

           The hand

                thick with measurement

         Weight of rain

                on clitoris testicles

There's thirty thousand feet of air between where I'm sitting and the Basin of the Green River. I never got a chance to tell you I thought your preference for shot guns was the close quarters ticket that'd get you back. You asked if I understood what it was like to watch the eyes of a man who gets a whole M16 clip emptied into his chest. You asked me other things too and let the questions trail off. About the forty mile bike rides we took to go swim the Santa Ana, explore the quicksand edged bluffs or the way we'd stand in the fields and have rock fights, play war, break all the windows of a no one at home house. Maybe your preference started the day we scared out rattlesnakes and then half disintegrated them with 30/30s. And I don't know what to say about the malarial hives you get or what you're gonna find after your second tour's done. You kept askin me if I knew what it was like and I could think about our conversation and who it could be told to. Could I tell it to my uncles who saw so much violence they couldn't be touched from behind for years after they came home by their children or wives. And what would they say I ought've said to you? Here's a little more of that red ochre I dug up. You said your recon unit started to call the whole country "The Slab." Don't go on it without this.

No call for help but the kind of message anyway luring the official contempts for temptation, a splash of seduction too, like the first white men to ever see the thighs of a Michigan, an Ohio some Jean Nicolet hovering above the human and non-human preferences of his assumptions about the feast and where to deliver his bite in a birch-bark canoe between Lakes Huron and Superior the decade before the Iroquois made the lands from the Ohio River to the shores of Lake Erie into a firing range perfecting their bodies for seventy mile a day war runs, ambush disciplines. There were no dreams of occupation, natural resources. It was a personal on-foot geography luring a brain map of home but all the sweep of that emptiness couldn't compare to a French Voyageur or one English ship carrying escaped house flies churning toward the innocent and the vaporizations about to enthrall a whole world in the new mysticisms of skinning camps in their unyielding everywheres slippery with fat and blood.

In April of 2004 Jeb Bush opened the "nation's first faith-based prison." What sort of debasement can this be especially as one re-hears the Florida governor's brother's statement in his 2003 State of the Union message in regards to the execution of either suspected or direct foes in "The War on Terror": "Let's put it this way," the ruler boasted, "they are no longer a problem." What Hell Rites have these two brothers entered and the pallor of their vocabulary carrying what infections?

Tuesday May 25th 2004: Bush in his confusion over Abu Ghraib offered in a speech given at the War College at Carlisle Pennsylvania (also site, it must be remembered of one of the nation's great tragedies where generations of Native American children were kidnapped and forced to assume the identity of "white people" – a scouring – the notorious "Indian School" and where also Clay and me, taking a father and son journey across America after his graduation from Oberlin College in 2000 saw the huge signs for Carlisle advertising the city as "The World Radio Center of Yewah"), to build a new American style maximum security prison as a gift to Iraq. One builds faith-based prisons based upon what possible forms of discrimination or embrace of religion and further what could a "faith-based" prison be or prison as a Democratic "Gift" to an invaded people?

April 26th 2004: Our friends, Robert and Penny, came for a local poetry festival called "Border Voices." It gave us the occasion, after many years, for a family re-union. Bob's art in his 77th year has achieved another depth charged with his advanced age, or is it his advanced youth? His great love of his children and grandchildren, his meeting people in the larger world, his teaching and the wonderful arousal of a humanity and language to express what now, in this horrible retreat from humanity America worships, find little occasion for. The poetry has a freshened versatility, free to roam over forms and gestures in thinking and feeling and probings which Gail and I found deeply encouraging and reassuring. "A Man Standing" containing himself in that ancient posture, not thankfully in his wisdom but in what is and has happened saying that the diversifications of hatred, suspicions, and corruption, the idealized embodiments and cravings for threat and violence are violating us all in ways that have no seeming end; we cannot, have no ability to fathom their leakage upon ourselves. Adrienne Rich, the other poet, is a lovely, present human being with profound courage. Is that enough? I think it is. The "art" has a lesser reach, is tenuous before the enormous infinity of language and creative expression where Robert moved unhesitantly toward these dangerous reservoirs. But her reality as a Person is one of precise rectitudes. There was a Q & A after-segment where Bob's and Adreinne's care for Daily Existence, for Poetry, and abiding regard for creaturely mindfulness and its practices was offered with a gentle homely grace that was deeply touching. This man and woman who have sharpened themselves in ways so rarely presented or cared for; the ancient traditions and longings that one demand something of oneself and hear with a profound difference. The last time we saw Bob.

Supreme Court hears arguments about presidential war powers; specifically the power to indefinitely incarcerate suspected American citizens without any due process provided by the Constitution. This policy duplicates the internal policy of the domestic prison complex where the feeding process begins at twelve; catch any kid male or female at this age and you've got an indefinite "client" you can turn into a permanent cash cow and at a certain not too distant moment no one will be safe from the kidnappings because of the Citizenry's desire to parent the disowning removes that make possible the ordination of carelessness, dissolution, and starvation of the actual bond with "appearances" human beings must have if the living contents of health are to be recognized. Otherwise how can we hear the reprimands of the dead who tell us, the living, of our catastrophic failure to live well together, that this is finally all we have – acephalous – are we the headless conjuring the neglected future?

Friday May 7th 2004: Our epiphyllums are in their silken almost angelic pink and white blooms. A relief. Such startling, reassuring beauty before the world-wide revelations of our darkest secret savageries and impulses. In light of this drudgery, this easily produced over-abundance (among all of our over-abundances!), of hate, there is this sad by-line in the news from "Joseph, Texas": the tombstone of a Black man who was dragged to death was found broken and with racial epithets carved into the granite. "We hoped he could rest in peace," said Stella Byrd, the mother of 1998 dragging victim, James Byrd Jr., adding, "They've done enough to him already." Byrd was on his way home from a party June 7, 1998, when he crossed the paths of three white men who had been drinking. The men took Byrd to a country road, beat him, chained him to their truck by his ankles and dragged him more than two miles until he was dismembered and decapitated. This also comes with the reawakenings of the sorrows of Emmett Till. What amazes here is not just the violation but the deeper carriages of language; that the overt or "real time world" is called "White" by Rumsfeld, Cambone Wolfowitz. The pallor infecting the vowels and consonants and who gets read into or out of the "Whiteness." The color scheme calls up Whitman's "Latent right of insurrection" to restore the Health of the People.

Friday May 28th 2004: Before Bush's promise to build American style maximum security prisons in Iraq might one consider how the inmate population had grown 2.9% domestically, and, in the year 2003, the numbers for the United States record the fastest pace for the previous four years:

State prisons:	1.8% Increase
Feds :	7.1% Increase
Local jails :	3.9% Increase

Ashcroft thinks the report " ... shows the success of efforts to take hard-core criminals off the streets. It is no accident that violent crime is at a 30 year

low while prison population is up . . . Violent crime and recidivist criminals are getting tough sentences while law abiding Americans are enjoy-
ing unprecedented safety . . ." Does "unprecedented safety" mean, as
William Bennett stated on September 29th 2005, "That if you wanted to
reduce crime, you could, if that were your sole purposes, you could abort
every Black baby in this country, and your crime rate would go down . . ."
What could this hero of conservative morality be saying on his Salem Radio
Network Show? Is the author of the "Book of Virtues" extending a warning,
a notice that we are all in danger? If one examines too, the vulgarity of such
suggestion and the forms of "hard core" safety which accompany it, then in
what frame are we to consider the new Streamlined Procedures Act submitted by senators John Kyl of Arizona and representative Dan Lungren
of California. The stated goal of the proposal is to stop the "endless delays"
between convictions in capital cases and executions. The American Bar
Association responded by pointing out that the bill "inadequately protects
the innocent by proposing virtually unattainable procedural and other
requirements to establish innocence. These requirements will prevent
many innocent prisoners from reaching federal court . . ." Is this information a "porn site" similar to either a "Camp Nama" (where American soldiers from Task Force 6-26 posted placards: "NO BLOOD, NO FOUL,"
reflecting their approach to torture techniques, "If you don't make them
bleed, they can't prosecute for it."), or to "NowThatsFuckedUp.com where
American soldiers in Iraq and Afghanistan have been photographing dead
bodies in various forms of mutilation, dismemberment, and gore? Along
with the images appear such captions as:

"What every Iraqi should look like"

"Bad day for this Dude"

the words an escort for bodies horribly ripped to shreds. The owner, Chris
Wilson, of Lakeland Florida, gives the American soldiers free access to
his porn site, one of the most popular in the military, in exchange for the
most gruesome images. "The Book of Virtues" along with the above
statement made by its author, "The Streamlined Procedures Act," and

"NowThatsFuckedUp.com," are each congregation ready lap dances TeachMeHowFeaturesofTheAdamandEveCollection'sDirtyDiapers PeeForMeOneMoreTime virtual HeShes only the present American wilderness can produce; a clairvoyant forlornness lying outside even the most superb visionary guesses.

Friday January 28th 2005: A cooling breeze makes our wind chimes sway. Still weeding our gardens, overgrown from the stay in Europe. Six months fertilizes seas of weeds. A fascinating letter appeared this week. Ramsey Clark offered to defend Saddam Hussein; an act of vigorous, but quietly stated personal courage, as the former attorney general stated: " . . . any court that considers criminal charges against Saddam Hussein must have the power and mandate to consider charges against leaders and military personnel of the U.S., Britain, and other nations that participated in the aggression against Iraq if equal justice under the law is to have meaning. No power or person, can be above the law. For there to be peace, the days of victor's justice must end . . ." Here the Jeffersonian rhetoric attempting to face the barrenness, the fulfilling intent of the official projections of THIS WARTIME for the next thirty-five to forty years written into the codes of public relations as an ecstatic fate to be shared. In this I hear Bassanio's soliloquy in "The Merchant of Venice"; not only the obscuring show of evil but the assumption of "valor's excrement"; one of the most, for me, vivid and nightmarish revelations of the sickness of rule which must disown reality:

"So may the outward shows be lest themselves;
the world is still deceived with ornament.
In law, what plea so tainted and corrupt
But being seasoned with a gracious voice,
Obscures the show of evil? In religion,
What damned error but some sober brow

Will bless it and approve it with a text
Hiding the grossness with fair ornament?
There is no vice so simple but assumes
Some mark of virtue on his outward parts.
How many cowards whose hearts are all as false
As stairs of sand, wear yet upon their chins
The beards of Hercules and frowning Mars,
Who inward searched, have livers white as milk!
And these assume but valor's excrement
To render them redoubted . . ."

Saturday January 29th 2005: Cool. A spectacular sky filled with billowing clouds letting in filtered sunlight. Muted colors. "By the time of the Second World War," Robert Duncan wrote in "Poetry and Strife," "I saw the reality of Hitler America was fighting as lying in what America was becoming. The United States would emerge as the power in Europe and Asia that Germany and Japan had been. I had formed a mystical pacifism: All national allegiances – my own order as an American – seemed to be really betrayals of the larger order of Man. In time we defeated Hitler, and live now in a world where not only does Hitler spring anew in his home-ground which our war did nothing to transform, but we find our government more and more in his place. Butchering Germans and Japanese had not exterminated the will to power through terror but extended it . . ."
These words of Duncan's move into the continuously painful core of the unadmitted as Karl Rove assumes a propagandist triumph which proposes to re-cast the Republican Party as the anvil of "Civil Rights" via the "Freedom Calendar" assuming, fantastically, a major position in the struggle of Black People to gain equality.
" . . . But I am in /So far in blood . . ." Richard the Third stated in Shakespeare's tragedy and the central image of the play, the cruelty, fear, and murder not only of persons but the Nation lying for discovery still in

Queen Margaret's unbearable question which exactly pertains to our own dilemma:

"Why strew'st thou sugar on that bottled spider . . ."

Monday January 31 at 2005: Walked around Lake Murray. Cowles Mountain so iridescent one can see almost every geologic fold of this cretaceous knob. We weeded, straightened out the litter next to Gail's large gas kiln; readying for new fire. I've been reading Olson's "Call Me Ishmael" once more. The passages about the wide antagonisms in democracy – democracy as tragedy in Melville's sense derived from Shakespeare and Jackson: the cast of a "great man" and a whale ship reminded Melville of two things as Olson had it:

1. Democracy had not rid itself of overlords, and
2. The common man and woman however free leans on a leader:
   the leader however dislocated, leans on a straw.

Melville's vision of paltry and base "entrenchments" which must be renewed in order for a "leader" to achieve supremacy over other men. Certain "Sultanisms" as Melville so accurately located the language by which to gauge the presiding currents of this sea we are treading as Bush and his various counterparts; Milton Friedman, the Heritage Foundation, the Cato Institute, the Fundamentalist supervisors informing the nation's Black ministries that Social Security and its New Deal promises do not work for "Them" a constituency with a "shorter life-span" and because of that fated to receive fewer benefits. What sort of sales pitch is this? The authors of the Book of Wrongs playing upon the contents and ugliest depths making the American Bottoms into an even greater invasive and unlivable séance. Shakespeare said the "world's soul is hypocrisy." And we, being creatures of the full disorder, its enthusiasms, possessions, liables? Can one think of Shakespeare's "fact" within a context similar to that which Frank O'Hara proposes for John Keats as "insight into the structure of human sensibility" rather than as "truth"?

"The error," O'Hara said (and I think this applies to Shakespeare in the instance of what his dictum attracts), "the grievous one when approaching Keats is to think that 'Beauty is truth, truth beauty' that Keats was writing about poetry. His insight into the structure of human sensibility (if this seems tautological, one may remark on Rilke's insight into that of animals and angels) is more merely against the ugliness of lying than Mondrian is against paintings which do not affirm the horizontal and vertical..." Perhaps equal error is to assume that Shakespeare was discussing "soul" – that the prestige of the word itself poses a precariousness and confusion about the implacable formality of this knowledge invoked as a meticulous extremity, the perfect observation as a "hand-me-down" which Shakespeare himself refuses to covet. And knew as Olson about worlds leaning "on a straw."

Thursday February 3rd 2005: A Santa Ana has arrived sweeping sky of cloud and draining these coastal desert spaces of any residual moistures. Our jasmine and orange blossoms have begun to bloom; the backyard filled with perfumes. Dinner last night at Jerry and Diane's and their other guests, a roofer who had earlier done a job for them, and his wife, a mail order bride who, at one time, was Vladimir Putin's English translator when he was mayor of St. Petersburg. And the husband, a former competitive body builder who lifted weights in the same gym with the young Arnold Schwarzenegger. The night was filled with descriptions of Russia, the California governor smoking maryjane, and a portrait of Gorbachev through Russian eyes; a bungler, a dolt who speaks Russian with wooden teeth and tongue, held below contempt. An utterly different cast of impressions from the Americans who held him the hero of that moment.

Bush in his six years as governor of Texas signed 152 death warrants and granted clemency only once. He also signed legislation that placed curbs on death penalty appeals even though some defendants in this state were known to have been represented by incompetent lawyers. So the present trend at the federal level to "streamline" persons to the "Chair" or the "Gas Chamber."

Abu Ghraib/LA County Jail both facilities with thousands of prisoners, jeopardize all who enter through the gates. Abu Ghraib filled with rats, scarce edible food, little potable water, wild dogs, trash. LA County jail riddled with security flaws, understaffed, a threat to both inmates and guards.

Saturday February 5th 2005: We've entered into the strange, murky, unanswered questions Lawrence raises in his great essay about America and Americans – the terrible under-consciousness of America – the destiny to destroy. An American general, James Mattis, stated in front of a group at the San Diego Convention Center, "Actually it's a lot of fun to fight, you know. It's a hell of a hoot. It's fun to shoot some people . . . You go into Afghanistan, you've got guys who slapped women around for five years because they didn't wear a veil. You know, guys like that ain't got no manhood left anyway. So it's a hell of a lot of fun to shoot them." His comments were met with laughter and applause. The American executioner unleashed with the annulling hatreds of anything and everything that might stand in its way.

Alberto Gonzales ratified.

We've made violence so companionable it has become a kind of weather sparing nothing.

Monday February 7th 2005: Late start, sky shrouded in thick grey clouds, some sprinkles, some wind as our jasmine and orange blossoms continue to bloom.

Rocky Flats has re-arisen. From 1952 to 1989 the plutonium triggers for America's hydrogen bombs were produced here. The legacy: 14.2 tons of plutonium and 7.3 tons of uranium were buried in barrels which have rusted out, the materials leaked into the soil. The responsible corporation:

Rockwell International – was fined $18.5 million for "environmental violations." At least one building on the site was called "the most dangerous structure in the country" by the Energy Department. Federal officials say the plutonium and uranium levels are "acceptable." Plutonium has been in the atmosphere since the nuclear testing began. These background levels of radiation have been officially designated as "normal."

The face of the world after the disappearance of Being made available for occupancy yet lifted slightly from it is support.

Thursday February 10th 2005:
The random violence in the United States included today news of a scalping which took place in Boise Idaho.

I have been trying to think of these recordings in terms of a refinement of Blake's "Songs of Innocence and of Experience Showing The Two Contrary States of The Soul" but these vocabularies are a brutality so unattached to anything we have been able to know or to admit that they will not function as soundful music certainly as Blake composes and invents. The involuntary blank, for instance, of a person caught in open unprotected space at the moment of a single rapid pulse at thermal maximum of nuclear blast, the total energy received when no evasive action is possible, and when then a person might blink as simple automatic nervous reaction and have the eyes burnt to a sightless blister at that moment and can we regard such legend which now lies in the hidden repositories of the "normal" as part of the variation in the expected effects and their yields as we attempt to think about the Biblical Empire of the "Ownership Society" which spreads at 2 calories per square centimeter with its second or third degree burns and can there be any way not to look at the Fireball?

Tuesday February 15th 2005: The Bush administration intends to suppress a billion dollar settlement granted to a group of "Gulf War" pilots captured and then tortured in the Abu Ghraib prison. The money, won from the country of Iraq, must be used for the purposes of this war.

Thursday February 17th 2005: Clouds thickening; the quietudes of pre-rain stillness upon land and air. Fossil skull finds from 1967 in the Omo River Valley in Ethiopia have been newly re-analyzed. This more recent data places the ages of the two artifacts, anatomically modern human skull caps (Omo I and Omo II) at 195,000BC. The analysis is extremely important; the re-dating of these fragments goes directly to the issue of the origin of our species and the timing of that event in the evolutionary nursery in East Africa. If these are the divinatory objects of our origins then what other durations are there waiting? I think of Rimbaud, the first European explorer to have looked out on these tangible spaces, walked this ground carrying his Cro-Magnon curiosities and a question that for me haunts his "Illuminations": the possibility that the experiment of Hominidae may be filled with one or two ghost forms which had the potential for far more awareness than ourselves, and we may be, merely an "average" or worse whose prevailings keep such inquiries at bay and that his art reached for precedents of inquiry; what lies beyond the hedge pushing at the future of intelligibility and price for the sake of the precariousness, the "artistic vigilance" to use here Frank O'Hara's terms. And what to do with these Omo Persons? Perhaps they are a part of phenomena having to do with "That –One-You-Are-Speaking-About" who reappears as a Sign of Existence's ruin, the Messenger known all over ancient North America in the form of a hairy giant roaming the shadows, a being of powers, dangerous to even see. Are these fragments of weir beings whispering to us and can this distance be measured by a shout, span from forefinger to thumb, the length of a good or bad night's sleep, the intervals between the letters of particular words, the weight of ten pseudo-prophets and the end-vowels of their lies? The initiation of the spell we are living through, I think in large part begins with the prisons and their will to perpetuity. The fact that each site must be regarded as lasting a century and more; a century, for instance, in these decades can be considered an eternity but yet no eternity contains the awesome life suffocating space of one second locked away in steel and within that "pulsation of an artery" Blake materializes lies our politicians taking amorous delight in virginal delusions represented by the facts this week (November 6th through 13th 2005) of the CIA's "Black Sites" and the members of congress falling into incoherence not over the existence of these torture camps but over the fact that their existence has been "leaked" – the all-purpose stand-in verb covering everything from the mysteries of plutonium storage to security breaches. The "sites," so isolate, have become acceptable highly financed real estates of dread which are transformed into enriched ores. Example: Marc Mauer's most recent study for the Sentencing Project focuses on the 1.5 million convicted felons who have completed their sentences, are "free" and are still denied the right to vote. Todd Graziano, director of the Center for Legal and Judicial Studies at the Heritage Foundation says, "It helps the rehabilitation process if you have to demonstrate worthiness." Since all forms of useful rehabilitation have been utterly censored from use in our prison systems what part of the process is Todd Graziano referring to? Further, what "worthiness" exactly rides this man's bad breath reeking of those racisms which desire most to control the voting booth. How does punishment become a replicating ingot wherever the punished who have served the legal terms of their punishment turn? And what is "worth" as it forms the foundation of new more quiet expert savageries and persecutions, the archaic estimation from which the word proceeds as alchemy of turning profits gaining speed? The phantom monstrosities of "safety" holding the lures of further obedience, conformity, purity, and "worthiness"; the last (or first) touch of visionary coin flipped into the forests of wrong colored souls in this Hell/ Play of words let loose in allegories glistening with neutron attenuation, neptunium threshold, equilibrium spectrums and their general applicability for any given region?

Saturday February 17th 2005: Bill Maher wrote an editorial yesterday referring to a new survey of post 9/11 high school graduates the majority of whom think newspapers should not be allowed to publish without government approval and nearly one in five stated that Americans should be prohibited from expressing unpopular opinions. Maher reminded his reader that Bush once asked. "Is our children learning?" and the answer: "Yes they is."

Thursday March 1st 2005: Intermittent sunlight, slight winds, our yard filled with odors of jasmine and orange blossom. Planted new fruit trees this weekend in our raised garden (two peach, one plum). Soil still soaked from recent heavy rains.
More information appearing about Abdul Qadeer Khan's network and sale of nuclear secrets, bomb production machinery, and instructions. This world criminal was watched for years by intelligence agencies in Europe, Russia, and the United States. What will I tell my grandchildren when they ask about who allowed this one person the Death of the World Game to be a voyeurism of such sweeping amplitudes; to so blatantly compromise planetary life. These powers watching themselves watch and wait, gawking, sex-gaming and polishing world murder?

Monday March 7th 2005: Atmosphere beginning to warm. Orion and Pleiades setting earlier. Birds coming out as well, and newer leafage.
The California prison system once more; capital punishment and Death Row inmates who stay in these cages for decades. 640 Death Row residents or 20% of the nation's total costing at least a $100 million per year, this

dallying with morbidity, repellence, and decomposition; the ransom of chastities. Thinking of the opening lines of Ginsberg's "Kaddish":

No more to say, and nothing to weep for but the Beings in the
    Dream, trapped in its disappearance,
Sighing, screaming with it, buying and selling pieces of phantom . . ."

The poet's " . . . pieces of phantom . . ." with this shocking inviolate status granted to it. The intermingled mass of sex, glamour, ritual executions waiting in a trembled orbit, the Domination of these objects of fear, and the caged themselves knowing that no exorcism is any longer possible because of the horrible intimacy their "Fact" known or unknown, it no longer matters, has come to, a kind of seething lava dome expanding and contracting, the store of Death.

And another scandal out of Atwater Prison north of Modesto where convicts are re-cycling used computers but with no safety standards. The people are exposed to dusts from lead, cadmium, and barium. Any "long-term" exposure (and no one knows what that length of time is) to these metals causes kidney damage and risk of lung and prostate cancer. Investigators found the work site where the prisoners eat and labor covered with these dusts. Paul M. Schultz, the Atwater warden, refused to take any calls and has so far agreed to only "superficial" responses to the problem and plays down the safety risks. The venture is part of UNICOR, division of the federal government that uses prison crews in business ventures and operates an expanding number of computer recycling plants in prisons nationwide, hoping to become a major player in the emerging business. Inmates can earn up to a dollar an hour breaking up machinery and sorting parts. The prisoners are allowed no safety standards and UNICOR refused to admit there is any problem. Is getting cancer in this prison industry a proof of worthiness?

Tuesday March 8th 2005: Daniel Pearl's parents, Judah and Ruth, were interviewed this morning on KPBS, NPR's local outlet. These people are not set on vengeance, but a focus on the children of the next generation with the hope of freeing all of mankind from the hatred and mercilessness which killed their son. They are setting up a foundation for conflict resolution and are calling for clarity and a way to free ourselves from the sickened darknesses. Before their plea, Tom Fudge, the interviewer, kept pressing this couple about revenge as if such refusal and sanity were incomprehensible, having no idea what further to ask or to say about the beautiful courage of this obviously stricken mother and father.

Sunday March 13th 2005: The number for California's prison population has jumped to 165,000. A record, (that number in late July 2006: 171,000 and along with this Governor Schwarzenegger is responsible for a 65% rise in the state prison budget in his short term) and as a record does the numerology represent a frenzy of decompositions into ghoulish "tolerance" on the part of the courts and the electorate? What vocabulary could allowably explain the overcrowding, filth, the danger, the lying, and the public relations involved in this unfolding worship of an even more swollen parasite filled with these freakish details masquerading as the normal? As example, Pat Roberts, the head of the Senate's Intelligence Committee is attempting to dismiss the CIA's abuse and complicity along with Vice Admiral Albert T. Church who has found that interrogation policies were not responsible for abuses and that independent investigations are not necessary. As Olson said:

> "now like Leroy and Malcom
> X the final wave
> of wash upon this
> desperate
> ugly

> cruel
>
> Land this Nation
>
> which never
>
> lets anyone
>
> come to
>
> shore . . ."

and this information so vital to the Life of the Nation will never be allowed landfall.

Thursday March 17th 2005: Pat Roberts, Chair of the Senate Intelligence Committee is blocking any more reviews of the interrogation and detention practices at Abu Ghraib and in Afghanistan. He wants no more formal investigation by his committee. Here is Rumsfeld's challenge that the world will witness America come to terms with these episodes with a full public and governmental accounting. Where in this process does anybody begin to define these acts as treason?

"Mein Kampf" has again become a best selling book and where? Turkey. Is "amazement" the word? Or is it just the maze of dilations taking place, the irresistible weariness and embrace of barrenness, the stifling sneakiness gathering and gathering?

Saturday March 19th 2005: Cool, overcast; hard sprinkles. Not quite rain but ominous with threat of downpour. Heard a marvelous interview on NPR this morning with John Ashbery who is now 78. When asked about previous poems, he said the only times he looks at those works of a previous condition is in the context of a public reading. Otherwise, when he thinks of what he learned there can be equated to Analytical Cubism in terms of restructuring the language and then offering it up for examination – that this seems to be a continuous undercurrent that does not repeat itself. Asked secondly about "accessibility" the poet offered that he has been told the poems are not "accessible" but that he felt the work as an exploration of the private that the poetry is open to be read and that they do access the margins between the "public" and "private." The interview, though far too brief, presented a rare scale of fascinations and commentaries.

What is it Akmatova said about the act of conscience? Something about "Whoever doesn't make continual reference to the torture chambers all around us is a criminal . . ."

Tuesday March 22nd 2005: A blossom drenched morning. Took Gail to the surgeon's yesterday. She has a torn "meniscus"; the cartilage which insulates the section of her skeleton between the femur and tibia. A significant tear which requires surgery either this week or early next, and as the Doctor says, "The problem won't go away."
Bobby Short has died, the wonderful sophisticated singer, and so too Walter Hopps, one of the great "outlaw" curators in late twentieth century America. A gifted, prescient, sharp, sadly flawed man who was too vague before the details of art administration and angered the keyholders. The obit reminded me of early Cold War LA when the city council decreed that "modern art" was communist propaganda and banned its public display.

Friday March 24th 2005: Sunny, a quick breeze. Gail had surgery on her left knee yesterday. Techniques are so much more advanced. The procedure took about twenty-five minutes and the "site" is a local out-patient "surgery center" where even back surgery is done. The doctors told Gail that the operation she had on her spine 35 years ago just before we married and which resulted in a painful two week hospital stay would now require no more than an overnight observation, if that, along with an immediate regimen of walking. The process with far more advanced knowledge and very streamlined. A light dose of anesthesia, the cut invasive but limited. Last night no pain; today the knee aches, but tolerable (no vicodin).

A Tyrannosaurus Rex thighbone has been discovered in a remote section of Montana with still intact 70 million year-old soft tissues which have been described as "virtually" identical to those of the modern ostrich. The specimen had to be broken in half for helicopter transport and through this "accident" the tissues were discovered. The paleontologist, Jack Horner, speculates that because so many specimens are handled with obvious care to avoid breakage that many more such intact tissues may be present in this as yet unexplored record in museum collections. "Ostriches that died six months ago are producing structures that are similar to dinosaurs that died 70 million years ago," says Mary H. Schweitzer, one of the participating scientists. The article is accompanied by electron photos of the materials.

A new study just published by the Urban Institute and Harvard's Civil Rights Project has found that the high school drop-out rate for California students is at a catastrophic high.

The numbers:

57% of African Americans graduate

60% Latinos

70% Whites

84% Asians

The state's methods for articulating previous numbers has been found to be "flawed." This study has cast aside California's accounting statistics and the state has been forced to acknowledge that its methods are false particularly with the examples of the 2002 numbers which stated 87% of students graduated in that year, when, in reality, the number was a 71% graduation rate. What are the consequences for these numbers? UC Santa Barbara Education professor, Russell Rumberger, estimates that the 66,657 drop-outs reported by California in 2002-03 could cost the state 14 billion in lost wages over the student's lifetimes, and add 1,225 inmates to the state's prisons. The real costs could be far higher, he noted, because of the state's under-reporting of the drop-out data. The social costs are described as "huge." Lower wages, higher unemployment, poorer health, lower tax revenues, increased crime.

Monday March 28th 2005: Another rainy day. Took Gail to the surgeon's for post-op check up. She's doing well but needs physical therapy which sounds cautiously right. Easter Sunday we spent quietly. Gail rested and each day presents dramatic progress and healing. Ordered pizza for Easter feast and we made a delicious salad. Lovely!

Abdul Qadeer Khan is in the news once again. The World Criminal is now under the protection of the Bush administration which has stopped any investigation of Khan's arms sales and technology purchases with the government of Pakistan. Gary Milhollin, a nuclear non-proliferation expert, called the policy by which Pakistanis get away with nuclear smuggling because we think they'll help fight terrorism "bizarre."

An article in the L.A. Times: A turning toward possible rehabilitation programs in the California's prisons. The new legislation is called the "Second Chance Act" which originally was initiated by a Kansas congressman but for this state the blue prints for reform are sketchy and funds are even scarcer. Moreover, one of the few initiatives that Schwarzenegger already has lauded – the diversion of non-violent parole violators into community based programs instead of prisons has begun to falter before it has had a chance to find infant's first breath. America has never trusted the possibility of rehabilitation but the present hatred and contempt for any prison reform begins with Robert Martinson's study for the New York State Legislature in 1974. I think the following excerpt from Jerome G. Miller's essay, written for the Washington Post in March of 1989, will help to explain who Robert Martinson was:

"Late one gloomy afternoon in 1980, New York sociologist Robert Martinson hurled himself through a ninth floor window of his

Manhattan apartment while his teenaged son looked on from across the room. An articulate criminologist, Martinson had become the leading debunker of the idea we could 'rehabilitate' criminals. His melancholy suicide was to be a metaphor for what would follow in American corrections.

On January 18, 1989, the abandonment of rehabilitation in corrections was confirmed by the U.S. Supreme Court. In *Mistretta v. United States*, the Court upheld federal 'sentencing guidelines' which remove rehabilitation from serious consideration when sentencing offenders. Defendants will henceforth be sentenced strictly for the crime, with no recognition given to such factors as amenability to treatment, personal and family history, previous efforts to rehabilitate oneself, or possible alternatives to prison. The Court outlined the history of the debate: 'Rehabilitation as a sound penological theory came to be questioned and, in any event, was regarded by some as an unattainable goal for most cases.' The Court cited a Senate Report which 'referred to the 'outmoded rehabilitation model' for federal criminal sentencing, and recognized that the efforts of the criminal justice system to achieve rehabilitation had failed.'

But had they?

Robert Martinson's skepticism derived from his role in a survey of 231 studies on offender rehabilitation. Entitled, *The Effectiveness of Correctional Treatment: A Survey of Treatment Evaluation Studies,* it was to become the most politically important criminological study of the past half century. Ironically, though the survey came to be virtually identified with Martinson's name, he had joined the research team only after they were well into their work. Senior author Douglas Lipton and co-author Judith Wilks found themselves eclipsed by Martinson's flamboyant personality and flair for the pithy in capsulizing his version of the meaning of an otherwise rather dry tome. His views were enthusiastically embraced by the national press, with lengthy stories appearing in major newspapers, news magazines and journals, often under the headline, 'Nothing Works!'

Paradoxically, the idea that nothing worked in rehabilitating offenders appealed to Left and Right alike. In an unusual four part series in the liberal *New Republic*, Martinson wrote, 'the representative array of correctional treatments has no applicable effect – positive or negative – on rates of recidivism of convicted offenders.' In the conservative magazine, the *Public Interest*, he wrote, ' . . . rehabilitative efforts that have been reported so far have no appreciable effect on recidivism.'

This was good news to civil libertarians concerned with the injustices of indeterminate sentencing. (In California, for example, offenders were routinely given 'day-to-life' prison sentences with release dates tied to such vague rehabilitative criteria as 'attitude'). But if the idea that 'nothing works' was well-received by liberals, it was even better news for conservatives who demanded tougher handling of offenders. But, to a nation emerging from the Vietnam War and an unruly youth and drug culture, 'nothing works' was a slogan for the times . . ."

How is one to regard the cometary, ever dilating lunge of Martinson's body over the Body of America?

One can on the basis of such information more clearly see in these precedents how the groundwork through specific domestic procedures in both Supreme Court Rulings and propaganda (though I don't think this single term any longer evokes the actual application of, to use Blake's terms, "Delusion" or "spices of sweet odours" and "stupefactions" and where Blake in his prophetic upheavals addresses "America" in "the dark land of Cabul" and asks "why Euphrates is red with blood . . ." extending his

"America A Prophecy" into the visionary depths of "Jerusalem") has been laid for the practices of indeterminate imprisonment as it pertains to the "War on Terror." Once netted, no release is possible either for our own minorities or for the threat-populations beyond our borders. Further, one can also recognize how routine such practices had become in our nation long before 9/11. We had as a people, to paraphrase Tocqueville, been prepared through thorough management, quietly and scrupulously over the decades of permanent war strategies, to accept and to perceive these betrayals as civic accomplishments extolling the public good rather than their reality of dictatorial compulsion hovering at the edges of modern democracy, restless and without cure.

Perhaps the tragedy of such an ugly suicide is based on what Martinson knew in that moment as he saw with increased horror the result of his "survey" and cajolings taken up as they were by forces he could not have anticipated and the absolute unbearable facts of the consequences he initiated and sadly came to understand as the destruction of millions of lives in this society. In our embrace of industrialized mercilessness have we become the dependents of an allowable fiendishness and in this embrace can we any longer understand where to begin to release ourselves from its hold? I think it is essential for us to recognize how this deadens a part of each of ourselves. It is at once portrait and crown jewel of a lifelessness we have begun to journey into and which we continue to thicken into a half-created darkness whose sediments we breath and eat and continue to birth. In this I remember Frank O'Hara's essay entitled "About Zhivago and His Poems" where this great American poet said " . . . Pasternak's epic is not the glorification of the plight of the individual, but of the accomplishment of the individual in the face of almost insuperable sufferings which are personal and emotionally real, never melodramatic and official. And it is the poet's duty to accomplish this articulation." In that O'Hara cites Pasternak's "Letters to Tula" and events which take place "on the *territory of conscience* . . ." as O'Hara co-identifies the "regions" of an actual person discussing not only why the poet must first be a person but "...the principles which were later to seduce Mayakovsky..." and which "...had been exposed in 'Letters to Tula' already...":

> ...I swear to you that the faith of my heart is greater than ever it was, the time will come – no, let me tell you about that later. Tear me to pieces, tear me to pieces, night, burn to ashes, burn, burn, brilliantly, luminously, the forgotten, the angry, the fiery word 'Conscience'! Burn maddening, petrol-bearing tongue of flame...
>
> This way of regarding life has come into being and now there is no place on earth where a man can warm his soul with the fire of shame: shame is everywhere watered down and cannot burn. Falsehood and dissipation. Thus for thirty years all who are singular live and drench their shame, old and young, and already it has spread through the whole world, among the unknown..."

O'Hara demonstrates through his discussion of Pasternak how each poet, each artist, each *person* as he or she approaches this *territory* is either confirmed in the identity of being an artist and *person* or confirmed in being a "chimera." One cannot avoid the terrible question about that "everywhere watered down and cannot burn" "spread through the whole world" and how this affects the artist, the fate of art, and the civilizations out of which artists and *persons* emerge.

Tuesday March 29th 2005: Cool, masses of billowing clouds; last night temperatures fell into the 30s. Gail off to physical therapy for her knee.
The United States is selling F16 fighter jets to Pakistan. The planes have the capacity to carry nuclear bombs and it now appears, with the completion of these sales, the Bush administration lied about North Korea's peddling of nuclear secrets to Libya. That "sale" can be traced to Abdul Qadeer Khan and Pakistan. Who exactly are the world criminals standing

so fatally over us all, their hands made of Venus Light ready to choke out the Life of Being?

In William Blake's watercolor "Satan Exulting Over Eve" Eve is lying in the subtle openness of her mysterious, trance-like slumber pulsing with the gentle indifference of her sexual readiness. She is both tense and loosened in the rhythmic permissions of her breathing and her waiting as she tenderly lays for the Serpent who is wrapping his body tail first at her toes and heel knowing these extremities are also the erectile veil hovering at the border of her barely emergent dreams. The scales flex lightly at those edges as the Serpent separates her feet, then moves up through her ankles, calves, and thighs. Serpent fever gaining the sexual range of bones, wanting abdomen, spine. Arching over her sleeping body the Serpent's head's weight creases her breasts. Her right arm lies extended, the sinew of hand and wrist relaxedly bent by the full Serpent's prick gracefully lifting her lower back as her little finger curls over the hot rind. Is this Blake's Imaginative Excess and innovative archaism as well as a commentary on a prehistoric stage of politics having to do with the secret adversary, the secret police at the roots of "intelligence" and "intelligence gathering" as if at first ravishing and spreading the toes, the dread of the pun coiling in prevention of sedition and rebellion? And the singing honey bees swarming in Plate II in the "The Marriage of Heaven & Hell"; are they the chorus of the primordial women of whom Eve is a Daughter carrying the House of Prophecy, Incantation, Visionary Seizure, Dread, Helpless Incomprehensible Sex Joys, the constant care of Human Health? Is it they who stand at the Gates of Disease and the Descent into hungers for gore which emerge with the Druidic skills of the "City" and what haunts the background of civic power and corruption? Who are the Giants who formed this world into its sensual existence and is this one of the ancient hovering questions which can once again emerge in this time. How does Blake render permanent the contents of inspiration where all forms of safety are spurned and through that drop every pretense of codified reference and description for the ordeals of rage and inspired delirium? The rise of the Gloomy Nations: America perfecting all the previous sickness emanating from spilled blood. The vast wheels of disease, hunger for minerals, and the genocides needed for the extractions. Does this image bring us into the proximities of Blake's most dangerous challenge. And who are the Ancient of Ancients Lawrence refers to, the ravishing murmurers with the voices of bees washing the skeletons of dead Gods?

The exaction. Shame with its talons, its fastening abstractions providing intensity and license to his sexual desperations and the charities he sought from them; devise the appropriate mask so the consuming arousal in his eyes would not bleed out and deliver him. He knew he was mourning for his sanity on those prolonged Downriver drives submitting to them wordlessly as he might have another man excited by the pure sullenness which he thought completed him and made him feel chaste. He would come then as a friend in the triumph of his chastity asking casually if anyone were interested in a lunch of Greek salad or pita bread using the day as protection. He thought of these transactions as a resting place where his body hovered either just before birth or immediately after death as if for this little while an amnesty could be generated; talk and his previously familiar voice returning to the hole in his head where it had singularly lurked but now wanted passage anywhere out of or into his body probing sometimes terribly sometimes tactfully, charming him with pain and pleasure as a wonderfully radiant "moth" for want of other assumptions of what it might be coming as it had, in the beginning, to the palms of his hands, and to rest there, if he would let it, while he slept. It would only ask that, only a request, the voice bearing childish affections. But it wanted more, slowly. He thought at first to raise his opposition. But it ate his opposition, revealed him, let him feel miraculously unbroken.

Wednesday March 30th 2005: An exceptional day. Hummingbirds searching our gardens, plants in bloom. David just called to tell me Robert Creeley, has died.

Not "God" not ever, but only men and women, as Lawrence said, who will "change the world, to make it free, more alive . . ." Bob was one of those "Men" inviting all of his friends to participate in being "more alive" and HERE, and HERE only to share it. Nowhere else; to cast oneself not only into a nerve of Being, but to actually want residence in existence, to be only one of the participating creatures, and not send the Others away, else come to the truly waiting and terrible loneliness if somehow we insist and murderously will the World to be exclusively for ourselves. What a drag not to hear his living voice ever again.

Saturday April 2nd 2005: Spring days are bringing their gifts of warmth, flowers, the graces of these births and renewals. Drove to Pomona California to see the works of Suzi Singer, a very gifted, and, for the most part, forgotten ceramicist from Germany. Her personal story is one of wrenching sadness. A Jewess born in 1891, she suffered from the extreme plagues of malnutrition during and after World War I. The result was catastrophic for her physically; she was permanently crippled by the want of food. Married a non-Jew, an Austrian miner who was killed in a mine accident in the 30s. With that tragedy what illusions of protection she might have had before the growth of Nazism vanished. An application for a visa was granted. She arrived in LA, became involved in the local pre-World War II Southern California community and made a very subtle and compelling art; figures almost "faery –tale" like in their beatific simplicities of the "every day" rendered with a tender unprotected emotional detail that ultimately was buried by the emergence of the abstract expressionist clay movement led by Peter Voulkos, Gail's great teacher/mentor. Singer's work has been stored away in the basement of Scripps College in Claremont, California since 1955. Before the disregards, the finalities of "historical" judgements, this brave woman's work re-emerges. The direct presence of the materials unimpeded by "stylization" and "smoothness" (Singer's terms), has as deep a ferocity as Peter Voulkos or John Mason. The release of the work from the dictates of modernist determinism present an art of gentle unrelenting dare, daring to remind us of the lifeless and unreal, as if the lifelessness were only One Week Old, as Charles Olson might say, and could be fished for and eaten raw and come to no rest.

There are two Appalachians. The older uplift starts in Pennsylvania and surges to Georgia and Alabama. An ancient journey to the south with a rolling upland to its east, a more elevated tougher approach to the west heading still from the Quaker dreams in to Virginia. The Folded Appalachians, the "Newer" as some called them, rise up from the folds of the St. Lawrence and migrate also toward the manatees, encompassing the Valley of the Hudson, and cutting Susquehanna, Maryland, Virginia, the Tennessee Smokies on through the Chattahoochee Forests and down into the Tallapoosa. Get a car even today, begin your climb at Carlisle, where the First People went to a crossroad and got their ancient identities kidnapped, and Pittsburgh, East Cadiz, though a twentieth century highway manicures the horizon, will begin to seem like the Kingdom of Og in Orion, the titty bars and bowling alleys remote as the spectre sons of the Father Druid, nine hours and a streak of downhill curves and valleys where the stranger given the wrong phone number on the right morning might still get to see his soul float in the smoke of Kentucky Long Rifle or the World Center of the Radio Assemblies of Yewah. On a good summer's day these mountains, though they don't seem higher than a moon eaten Sierra foothill, get more formidable with each inward and outward valley climb. Those surges of earth must have given the first waves of land hungry European pilgrims a mean short life with a Shawnee hatchet waiting for their sternums. The rivers dissecting these ridges still carry a lure and you could go there and become a wrong way Ophelia yourself carried by the

Charlotte, the Juniata, the Youhiogheny, the Cheat Vally Fork, or the Mohawk. Take a thousand mile slide into the Saluda till your bones crease the Eno, Hico, and Haw.

The legendary Long Rifle, though a frightening tool in the hands of an ice-eyed shooter, became another piece of cold metal, for the most part, before the ancient men who could melt away leaving a signature of hacked corpses and no provision of restorable sanity for those who sighted the leftovers. The presence of that mystical abandonment over fresh harvested lifelessness and blood cut new tributaries into the mind's districts beyond which even fear and terror hardly would go. The warriors, merciless, silent, painted in the erotic tides of their death skills were pitched slowly toward a decimate rage over land speculation and illegal settlement of their hunting grounds and rivers. The pressure of huge population increases, white women going to child early and constantly doubling every generation in the eighteenth century equaled two fatigues; worn out women and worn out land and the new extortions such an abyss could bear via who'd pull the primeval cherry and walnut timbers toward a version of scaling laws and their rules for transforming the effects of energy into the virtue of representative simplicity demonstrating how it must have seemed like the properties of blast wave between distance (theirs) and energy yield (ours), and the overpressure which still attains from the cube root of that ground zero on the shores of the great Ohiopeekhana, the "River of Many Whitecaps," the legendary blue of its waters, its islands, and the wild grapes hanging from its forests. How it all comes down to what the Dreamers may have seen in the widening precessions they could not allow into the hours in which they lived.

Gail baked a cake today in honor of Bob Creeley. A replica of the cover for "Memory Gardens" which we took to the San Diego Book Arts Coalition show at the UCSD library – we ate it and it was good, though Gail wanting it to be even yummier, doubted its quality.

Read about the rates of cancer in the United States. Fully ½ of all cancers are attributable to tobacco related products. Here the sanctioned "Pusher" honored, protected, fully murderous, abducting millions.

The number of "Detainees" in Iraq and Afghanistan has grown to more than 11,000 and the secrecy surrounding American detention operations has intensified says Bob Herbert of the New York Times. Detention Operations Inside/Outside; world become the spacemaster option project launched, phase management bidded, Guard Tower Manpower redeployed. Eyes that never close, ears that always hear must be of first quality. No excuses. Built to meet or exceed.

Land trafficking became the central hallucination, better than any branch of lawyering ever cooked on a spoon. If the Windigo hungered and slurped up lives, coiled in the heart of anything that pumped blood and dreams, though it was terrible and sure, it too was finally held to the raptures of the world. This other appetite seemed just to take the bars of creation, bind them to the trembling shades and twenty-seven folds of sexual immensities wound out of Albany, Philadelphia, London; "Vandalia" resistless as the first Euphrates hardened with its secret bodies groaning with their silver eyes and crystal fingers – the "Transylvania Company" sending out its flocks of vampires that might be flying still, thirsty for the ammonia seas of Jupiter. The use of contract and convict labor to open up lands for speculation fell on no principle anyway other than the blind fury of a Miami who slowly submitted those bodies to a roasting by the delicate application of embers, their two-thousand degree petals going back to the Caribbean when it was a mirror of whispers from one island to another about slaves, man-eating dogs, and the clouds hovering over a lagoon created by human meat.

Who rules these forests and lakes with their present factories and tides of poisons as if it were the menstrual spillage of the Ice Queens and to drink any potation here, water or turpentine as I had done might beget the reversal of languages and their florescences into a retreat to the two original wellsprings; the Holy Language, Hebrew, and the Utterances of Demons – those chariots waiting even now for the descent.

Wednesday April 6th 2005: Military recruiters are invading the high schools, not in wealthy neighborhoods, but the poor and marginal. Some attend PE classes, play in faculty basketball games, give hand-outs at lunches. They patronize, squeeze flesh, present themselves as "friends" and mentors; glad handing, becoming familiar as the Army's "School Recruiting Handbook" instructs. This "guide" tells recruiters "to deliver doughnuts and coffee for the school staff once a month; attend faculty and parent meetings, chaperon dances, participate in Black Heritage Month and Hispanic Heritage Month; meet with student government, newspaper editors and athletes, lead the football teams in calisthenics . . ." (to "deliver": the verb and its explosion phenomena are dependent on such properties of the medium as its temperature, pressure density, and composition). The booklet advises "Be helpful and so much a part of the school scene that you are in constant demand . . ." One recruiter, Marine Sgt. Rick Carlois, lures children with images of fancy motorcycles, houses, rolex watches, his Mercedes and "Sean John" clothes. Some high schools in their rush to complicity have forced hundreds of students to take the "Armed Services Vocational Aptitude Battery Test" – recruiters pitch the test to principles and counselors as a "career exploration and assessment exam" while the Department of

Defense uses the test as a tool to provide the military with "pre-qualified leads" along with the "No Child Left Behind" law which designates that the military must be provided with students' home addresses and telephone numbers. One female recruiter, particularly unrelenting, knocking on front doors repeatedly in LA barrios – angering and frightening families and neighborhoods in her quest for bodies and what she felt was her "right" to fill quotas said in an interview on NPR that "these kids" were going to die anyway whether on the streets or in prison, so they might as well die for their country in Iraq." The nation "tight as ice" as Olson might say, the cynical frozen thing beyond mark or bearing having come to this actual in-waiting "normality" with its calving glacier weighted in impenetrable obscurities. Shores of La Brea at High Tide, Mineral in Full Tilt, Quotas for Prisons and Iraq. The long sought for pure pathology:
"A. Coprolite"; no address. Fish Bone survival in the digestive systems of the Pig, Dog, and Man in that order.

Amiri Baraka said decades ago that "Fate is a luxury available only to those citizens with alternatives."

An eighteenth century thirty foot canoe was the equivalent to a modern "Peterbuilt." A kind of fresh water tractor for the long haul crew of six with its provisions and goods bringing a four ton and more dead weight upstream and down. Nobody went to it without skill, strength, a brace of mind equal to the elasticity of transport. Far back as 1780 Detroit had a propensity to name its vehicles. The trade demanded a genealogy beginning with the canoe, its more cranky sisters, the dugout and "bateaux" came then with a harder geographical prescription: "Susquehanna" "Mohawk" "Kentucky" "Mackinaw." If one of the later objects was named "Pontiac" with the best hood ornament and strings of chrome sexy as a swim suit calendar in another period it only designates a means of design for the rough work of the Lakes, their adjacent rivers and rapids where lulls might bring on such uninterrupted stretches of day that the unsuspecting looked upon the return of the general bad temper of the parts as a personal ransom. You'da thought too those earlier populations would'a known how to not to spend themselves down to a four dollar a second nub, a should be "once upon a time" lurking somewhere but those old Detroiters cleared themselves out before dawn and stuck to it as a frenzy in every direction father to son mother to daughter each the admiral of a bulldozer ripping an unfathomable mountain.

Thursday April 21st 2005: Editorial today in the L.A. Times: "The Death Penalty." California has the largest population of Death Row inmates. The cost per year to hold and feed and let this abyss fester: $114 million which neither includes the legal costs of further prosecution nor the necessary requirement to provide these men and women with legal appeals. This population has ballooned to these proportions because voters and lawmakers have given prosecutors the ability to seek death sentences in more circumstances than have ever been allowed. Where does this American deviousness begin? A deviousness gifted in prayer, devout in worship searching for its chasteness, the errors causing sadness and questions as to the Troubler, Satan, and his most awful and tremendous visitations, the wonders of the invisible world encompassing Guantanamo, Abu Ghraib, the total number of Americans who have gone to prison and the spray dome of damage numbering 40 or 50 million when one considers a count capable of rendering even the most miniscule truths about the collapse of families, communities, generations branded for long term, short term the floating genetics perfect for the floating detention?

Bounty for heads begins in the 1630s. The Puritans liked the dead stares of the Pequod and the simpler the addition the simpler the subtraction. The thirst spread acceptably to women. One Connecticut "Lady" started with Wampanog men, went to their women. Finished with children: six it is reported and praises for her civil contributions.

The English offered scalp bounty to Indians for other Indians then the French for the English then the English for about everything. If the empire was for fur anyway, then why not have it be all inclusive like an another kind of deliverance where, at last, it didn't matter what color you were as long as you brought in the right number of ears, preferably by the hundreds, and if not, then by the pair. Spread that appetite from the Little Madawaska to the fisheries of the Oronoco where enslaved Cherokee, Choctaw or Delaware dove in Piranha water for pearl. Governor Clinton of New York liked best the scalps of young Frenchmen. And the handsomest Seneca killers? No one's wrote yet whether he reserved those for his finest dresses or licked the paint off the torso of his white lover after dancing naked as the warriors over the locks of those Parisians gone three quarters wild themselves. Depending on the technique you could survive a scalping. I'd prefer to be dead myself. Especially if it was Iroquois doing the surgery. To hear that part of your body being tore away. Who knows how much revulsion that might cause?

It's like watching all the human dignity you'd be allowed for eight lifetimes grow into a poisonous lake. A Seneca warrior'd start about the middle of your forehead. Cut down and around the ears. Through the back of the neck. And then gradually up to where the race started. Pull the hair. Only enough to raise the skin, then peel. A person who lived years after the injury wouldn't even know about the slow necrosis taking place in the layers of the skull. The caries was patient, appeared subtly with the loss of blood, the outer filaments of bone going black, moistureless, the process sinking until a perforation appeared for leakage of brain. Get through those gates and you went from one fatal island to another. Some reports imply a piece of White civilization was a thing to be smelled for miles. A single blockhouse might've been more dangerous than anything or anyplace on that frontier. A traveler in search of shelter could experience a Kentucky fort as an unspeakable shithive; dead dog, hog and horse guts, human excrement laying to unnoticed fester where it'd all been dropped

" . . . the most filthy nauseous potations . . ." ever seen. When we consider the necrosis, the patient caries, the revulsions accompanying the audible sensations of your body being torn away with such deft incision are we describing the modern effects of both the prison and nuclear bombs industries upon the living body of this nation and its citizens, the life of its arts? Is it, when we look at those family album-like photos of Abu Ghraib, the outer filaments of our civic imagination in the process of becoming a sinking perforation traceable to this earlier scalpwork and as we attempt to dangerously examine because it is dangerous for us at this point at the beginning of 21st century to even begin to say that there was a lust to mutilate individual Indians among the Frontiersmen as a common and private technique of encounter along a wooded trail and that this mutilation has shifted to ourselves, the savagery sought for without recourse, an adroitness in reflex, the intimate catastrophe originating as a grand intensity moving forward sure in its portion of prestidigitations.

Major evangelicals "want to strip Court's funds." Tony Perkins, president of the Family Research Council and James C. Dobson, founder of Focus on the Family see as particularly "offensive" the Supreme Court's finding that executing minors is unconstitutional. They criticized justice Anthony M. Kennedy's majority opinion noting that the Republican appointee had cited the laws of foreign nations that Dobson said applied the same standards as "the most liberal countries in Europe."

> Shelley said at the beginning of his poem "England in 1819":
> "Rulers who neither see, nor feel, nor know,
> But leech-like to their fainting country cling,
> Till they drop, blind in blood, without a blow, -
> A people starved and stabbed in the untilled field,-
> An army, which liberticide and prey

Makes as a two-edged sword to all who wield,-
Golden and sanguine laws which tempt and slay;
Religion Christless, Godless – a book sealed; . . .”

And “To Sidmouth and Castlereagh”
“As from their ancestral oak
Two empty ravens wind their clarion,
Yell by yell, and croak by croak,
When they scent the noonday smoke
Of fresh human carrion: . . .”

And the question to be asked of both these supposed men of Christ’s
    Name:
“Are ye – two vultures sick for battle,
Two scorpions under one wet stone,
Two bloodless wolves whose dry throats rattle,
Two crows perched on the murrained cattle,
Two vipers tangled into one.”

And to consider the appearance of the late eighteen century noun
“Liberticide”; is it one of the flocks fording the intolerable and what could
not be trusted, the Constitution for instance, gratefully pulverized into
brackish leftovers nearly at the point of its invention bequeathing no work-
able truth on this side of the Atlantic?

Consider the town called Ludington in Michigan and its connection to a
great voyage and what happened in the American forests in the last thirty
years of the seventeenth century where Father Jacques Marquette died
with a map in his head the Indians had given him prior to setting out with
Joliet matching bend for bend the Mississippi they floated down streams
washed into it and what they’d see on those shores as the voyagers were
served a feast below the present site of Memphis beginning with boiled

cornmeal awash in what was said to be delicious fat. Fish came second fol-
lowed by a good sized dog. Fourth a helping of buffalo. The hosts were
superb whittlers particularly of cottonwood carving giant trees into
dugouts "of one piece fifty feet long and three wide . . ." holding thirty
fully outfitted persons. And below the Ohio orchards of white plum so luscious they initiated commentary lasting a century as those groves subsided
into legend and nothingness.

Or consider "Last Chance" Colorado in the earliest stages of the 21st
century as we might communally re-assign the future into a Waste
Management Doctrine enticing waste management companies to geographies of dead and about-to-be abandoned towns. "Empty Space" is now
too one of the new post-abandonment minerals as the civilization jumps
from the previously material to the doctrines of the Unborn and their syn-
cretic afterglows and shimmering fore-lures. "Empty Space" wedded to
"Waste Disposal" sites. "Clean Harbors, Inc.," out of Massachusetts bearing
the infection of the intricate Maggot Emblem in Blake's terms language has
become where all the Armies of Disease visible or invisible gather round
the civilizations of humanity as this newest surgery on words becomes
Extreme Death Sport artfully fixed and planted. Philip Retallick "Clean
Harbor's" senior vice-president, called "Last Chance" a "good fit" for
storage among other local "wastes"; the old uranium mine tailings and
other radio-active materials used to line Denver's streets in the early 20th
century. The determinate of America's health from these beginnings: the
first dregs of the Atomic Age and how dangerously has the Nation aged in
the first five years of the 21st century?

Saturday April 30th 2005: Lynndie R. England of Abu Ghraib, barely 22
years old but already having done unalterable damage, is claiming for her
defense an extensive history of "mental problems" "handicaps" and "severe
learning disabilities" along with bearing and now birthing an out-of-
wedlock child by Charles R. Graner, the other smiling face in these images

"is here, fixed/forever . . . no release from the shabbiness" no cormorant to fly high enough out of Olson's living eye "February 7th 1966."

Cassandras could appear in those forests once in while too. A forlorn horseman riding up a meadow carrying that whisper on his breath that'll stick to no mind. Had the Shawnee known about the ancient Mediterranean grievance over mortal women and the hatred of their intelligence, where the Dardanelles bleed over the story of every girlhood from that moment forward, they might've taken pity on the man and his warnings. Even the God who thirsted and was repulsed by the beautiful faraway girl. They might not'a started with the smallest bones in his feet working sideways from the arches up, finishing with a miniature sea of blister below ankles to let the Immortal know to keep away. They't've, to get him over his petulance, taken him down to "Caintuck" to hunt black bear in that beautiful country kept purposefully free of humans, spent a month or two, combed his hair in the grease of that Ursus migrating up and down the Cumberland too, for two million years and eaten by the cheetah-like hyenas that cackled over landscapes from Florida to the Carrizo Fault stretching the continent toward another water breaking where F16s arc through supersonic dives into panicked herds of three-toed gazelle horses layered in the rarefacted obsidians cutting time and bathed him in that Tour of Wonders in the Licking River. Licked him good so's he'd dream himself back into his own previous business, sent him on his way dressed in a robe of turkey feathers for fashion and allure unlike anything an Aegean God ever imagined as actual mortal dress, become so pretty he'd go and forget about being rejected by delicious girls who are gonna die anyway, leave them to their worlds. But what could any Cassandra, especially a white man on a horse, do before those warriors who traveled to London or Paris one year, and the next up on the Wabash even hungrier for the arrangements of shadows that had repulsed and devoured them since a beginning even their most attuned clairvoyants were afraid to inhabit. The warrior who chopped you

alive out of your toenails might've been the keenest dresser, the one setting
the French or English Courts to high alert over trends, elegance. Silk hand-
kerchiefs for the forest gentleman perhaps enhancing arm bracelets, neck,
a flash of color held to tenuously exotic material, the last object the eyes
of the murdered saw clearly before the nothing dug for little morsels
there of brain light. Just the basic procedures. Laparotomy, Metal fragments filling intestines. X-rays of lumps in a void. "Expectant" asking if
they were gonna be alright with their minds leaking into a puddle behind
the ear. "Expectant" as if you were expected into the base regions of number
probability, fitted now to "kill ratio" but immune from all the other epi-
demics. The margins of cholera, polio sucking at the net, you preventative
at one end, and nauseants causing skeletal inversions in the womblife of a
country you'd slogged through at the other. Small pox hovering over the
first issuance of paper money and paper war spreading permanently into
unretrievable ornaments of perfection. Seemed like the Ohio was spotted
with a thousand Noah's Arks on those spring thaws in the 1760s. Pigs, a
chicken or two, horses along with five people on the River Oyo. Vines of the
still too faraway summer grapes hung with icicle as the human cargo, a
bunch of new Adams and Eves and their animals carrying the identities of
things to come calculated how long it'd take to get from Hannastown to the
"Big Bones" where the British Museum extracted Mastodon as token of the
flashiest dead and Equus coming back to the continent of its origins
wounded by the ball of a Wyandot musket went to death thrash, those hoofs
on a keel boat a spectacle to be watched from shore only as other passen-
gers rather than be turned to pulp dove into the ice wrapped water or waited
for the Shawnee to shake hands with the left over alive or dead crying out
"How dee doo!" How dee doo!" in the exact speech formation of the settlers
as they went about the seaming of finest scalpwork. Kickapoo or Wea
dressed as white men and speaking an unflawed English learned on the
streets of New York, Albany, London baited rivercraft and nothing was
spared in the lineages of carrion that came to seem ordinary as those goblins
waited on the shores of the Ohio. Women, their smallest children, yearling

men floated easily as chairs and cattle as testimony to the magic of true shape changing and the nameless Shadowy Mother vibrating at the Gates of Murder. Atrocity between settler and Indian created a rush but not for gold. It was a sort of fatigue growing through a moisture of rape, social collapses, and swindle where settlers, after they'd worked on the Cherokee, began to hunt each other and to cultivate that breakage as if any previous world had been only a mouse leaving in its passage the faintest burrow.

Wednesday April 7th 2005: Mary Dann, the great Shoshone land activist, has died standing against the oceans of deceit and greed, pillaging and evil; died as her niece Patricia Paul said "as she would have wanted with her boots on and hay in her pocket..."
There is a small photograph in the news today – a marine corps forward operating base being swept over by a sandstorm somewhere near the Syrian border. The "base" looks like a re-creation of a small suburb with sidewalks, streetlamps, decorative plants with a razor wire horizon. The insistent mountain of logistics, the belligerent need to create a fantasy world of convenience – intoxicating, pitiful, dutifully joined to the rules of hilltop McMansions.

May 3rd 2005: Lynndie England has been found guilty on this same day of Kenneth P. Clarke's obituary. The pioneering social psychologist and first Black man to be granted a full professorship at CCNY. Both he and his wife did the groundbreaking works on the consequences of segregation for Black children and that labor was crucial to the 1954 Supreme Court ruling outlawing segregation. But in later life, however, Clarke's outlook on race relations in America grew increasingly sour and dark. He looked upon the great work of his life "as a lost cause" – "My life has been a series of glorious defeats."

May 4th 2005: Lynndie England's defense lawyers are asking for leniency. The argument: a psychologist testified that the accused "was oxygen deprived at birth." The further results: "speech impairment and trouble learning to read . . ." How is one to gauge such information? Are we in one of Blake's "States" or "Ages" of "Dismal Woe" where the Sexual Texture of Humanity is ripped to shreds and vapours of howling sicknesses in the "nights of prosperity and wantonness" as the whirlwinds of deceit are let loose to vibrate the Looms and Webs of Death? Why Blake's imagery once more? Because his examinatory rage places unbearable imaginative pressure on the infectious pastes of dissimulation and the disconsolate labyrinths of perfected "hypocritic holiness." This dissection is the "Printing Press of Los" or the Bard's "War on Earth."

Saturday May 7th 2005: David Antin read last night at D.G. Wills Books. A fine presence of humor, cultural commentary, linguistic meditation, and courage to talk oneself through talk into thinking and what spontaneous thinking might be and is around the homely campfires of truth and delightfully reckoned and wandering and unafraid humane intelligence which announces how exactly boredom and stupidity bring each of us one hour closer to death. Before the piece we talked about our feelings toward Robert Creeley and the quality of friendship he was always able to step forward into, unprotected, vulnerable, with a grace unlike anyone we've ever known. The way he was able to step through and give courage, care, fresh ways to imagine life, home, the breadth of homely struggles and how one might touch and be touched by those struggles incisively where they matter most – never wanting or directing himself to public power, never a program to be the central issue as that most telling instant, when, years ago talking to Allen Ginsberg about the then possibility of initiating what was to become Naropa Institute Bob responded to Allen's proposal "Why start another institution when the whole fucking world is nothing but an institution, Allen?" This cutting the nets of anyone's personal vagueries sometimes at great cost and torment – the unrestricted invention of care and concentration on care so wonderfully, peculiarly, anguishedly. No distance. No guarantee. No safety. No decrepit cheat. To dispel the sickened residues which accompany the suffocations of all our lives with the actions of a new scrupulous working through to clarity;

"It's impossible that a man should be only a fact in himself"
Bob once said in response to a question of Linda Wagner's. And to spend one's life drawing the poisons out of and withering that "fact" and the peril it has brought to the world.

Reading W.G. Sebald's "Rings of Saturn" once more and the opening passages about "the source of Flaubert's scruples": The passage refers to a friend of Sebald's, Janine Dakyns, a lecturer in Romance languages whose "profound understanding of the nineteenth century French novel" touched the author deeply of which he comments: "Gustave Flaubert was for her by far the finest of writers, and on many occasions she quoted long passages from the thousands of pages of his correspondence, never failing to astound me. Janine had taken an intense personal interest in the scruples which dogged Flaubert's writing, that fear of the false which, she said, sometimes kept him confined to his couch for weeks or months on end in the dread that he would never be able to write another word without compromising himself in the most grievous of ways. Moreover, Janine said, he was convinced that everything he had written hitherto consisted solely in a string of the most abysmal errors and lies, the consequences of which were immeasurable. Janine maintained that the source of Flaubert's scruples was to be found in the relentless spread of stupidity which he had observed everywhere, and which he believed had already invaded his own head. It was (so supposedly once he said) as if one was sinking into sand . . ." Flaubert's "dread": Is he the first to discern the species/civilizational tide, the first to hear the surf of this ocean crashing at the edges? Scruple in terms of what the ancient Latin seems to propose; the quality and skill of "shredding" the mind for the sake of care and conscience, the painstaking work of a careful regard for the sustaining of being. Resistance. The spread of the new more modern stupidities, festering, germinating, racing the flesh like as to a school of flying fish bursting in lean flight on a momentary sun, the flutter tense, fathomless, inviting even a planet to sink away now from view or memory that on occasion might still be illuminated by Mars or Venus light, coming out for that moment from its nearly fixed place in evil, or, perhaps it is the one star in the Pleiades, in these centuries grown so faint no eye can any longer hold it or its echoes.

And the President whose Air Force One was seen in a near strafing pattern over Illinois as it came down for Adlai E. Stevenson's funeral had just authorized a mission of "Search and Destroy" – the combinations of those Etowah mannequins and Thich Quang Duc with his gasoline soaked body bubbling in a Saigon intersection, all three in the same lotus position were mixing in the clairvoyances of his mother's Mexican-Indian dreams.

Monday May 9th 2005: A story today which calls up "Project Ploughshares" that "brainchild" of Edward Teller's to use atomic weapons for civilian purposes and Cold War utopias. In this case a 40 kiloton explosion on Colorado's western slope to be detonated for a Texas oil company to get to a rich natural gas vein locked in the subterranean geology. Both the company and the government insist there is very little possibility for harm. The coupling of the explosion energy with the ambient medium. The energy of the motion of the mass of residues – fission products and other weapons materials moved outward at a million degrees per second as first a compression wave and then a steep fronted shock wave – the surfer dreaming of such excited states may still be attached to nuclei but within a hundredth of a microsecond or so may find that his atoms are stripped by the several tens of millions degrees pulsating either under the town or under the backyard as that new Hades becomes a soft x-ray region incinerating every previous attempt to say of Hades that it is now a harrow or plow — the evocation of and what joins it to say the electrical plugs for "Little

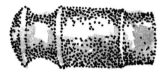

Boy"; the two: one red, one green and what are these colors as the pronouncement of the variations of the luminous in time after as seconds radiating into the variations of the apparent so that

in its previous variations becomes only one unmasking of the isothermal sphere aged 11 milliseconds (0.011 seconds) as the Xibalbans paddle their canoes over the seas of the yet to be whispered verbs for sustaining life.

Where could she give herself over completely without the stain of the contract and its estate? Grow to tremble and hover in the safe keepings archly draped in the studied wishlessness of the before and after women joined suppliantly to their shadows as a drained contrivance which was part of an earlier harvest looming over the glutted future in the 1700 decision at Montreal to burn hundreds of thousands of beaver pelt, the hard constricted bales resistant at first to the torchings, but gathering, the energy of the huge fires stinking horribly, their greasy blackened smoke staining the Great Lakes and the Plains beyond with market protections that would include, among its spoils, the sovereignty of appearances which surrounded her.

Tuesday May 10th 2005: A lovely morning filled with bird song and nest building; buds are out on our fig trees, as well our artichokes and vegetables. A small and nearly buried story in the LA Times: "Marines recall body armor after quality is questioned." The Corps is recalling 5,277 "combat vests" issued to troops in Iraq, Afghanistan, and Djibouti. The original report and questions over the vests appeared in the "Marine Corps Times" citing several vests manufactured by Point Blank Body Armor Inc., which fell short of Marine standards during testing in 2004 . . ." The further confluence of prisons, foreign policy, pornography. "Point Blank" is also a major player in the prison industry and advertises:

"Point Blank Corrections Armor:
Don't Get Stuck With Anything Less"
Or, for the purposes of privacy
associated with any of your own personal wishes
to get "Stuck" go wherever you want
for as long as you want
cook in the kitchen
whenever you're strippin
the bored and busty housewife

limo ready
casino hot
tough as they come
tease as you please

two is always better
than one
pregnant 2nd trimester
but still looks sexy
respecting limitations
if you love to see
petite feet.

Wednesday May 11th 2005: More on California's prisons. U.S. District Court Judge, Thelton Henderson, who personally visited and observed the health care "procedures" at San Quentin has "taken a major step . . . toward seizing control of California's prison health care system . . ." Judge Henderson's conclusion comes "Three years after California prison officials settled a class action lawsuit over inmate care by agreeing to make ambitious improvements. Despite that agreement, Henderson concluded and the state corrections officials acknowledged recently – the prison health care system continues to put convicts' lives in danger." Further: Corrections Undersecretary Kevin Carruth told lawmakers "that nothing in the report was overstated." Carruth also said officials have all but abandoned hope of providing health care on their own. In addition: "The union representing the doctors has sued to block steps the administration says would improve the quality of its members and remove those who are incompetent . . ."

On this same day the Army has called for "a one day halt" in its recruiting activities which includes 480 allegations of improper conduct by Army recruiters desperate for numbers. Recruiters have used the threat of prison, provided laxatives for weight loss in order to pass the military physical, and instructed potential signees on the ways to cover up past drug use.

What land would turn its gods into these rocks, lube it with the secret wet life of all the species stuck there, and you'd still come up with a remnant. The plains of pebbles marking the lower slopes below Gold Mountain are survivors, got uplifted with the San Bernardinos, and are little patches of what the terrain looked like seven million years ago when the pronghorns had to run seventy miles per hour and the dogs that hunted them were half hyena or half bears, evolution wavering, the wisps of it held in the hedgehog cactus flowers and the delicate remoteness of their petals. I picked one. Took a handful of the surface from another world and threw it into the glove compartment of my Merc. One of my childhood friends had walked into the jungle after throwing a captive out the door of a Heuy while he was still alive enough to disapprove of the fall. I didn't have a picture but I knew this one was wavering and if he was like those pebble plains with its dwarf flowers burned down to natural selection nub, the maintenance of that geological identity tearing into the brains of the living, then maybe the waverings of such friends and the ghost dogs still howling in the classified sections of the local strata had finally intersected.

NASA's "Swift Spacecraft" has captured what scientists believe to be the "birthcry" of a black hole caused by the collision of two neutron stars a billion light years from Earth. These bodies have contracted into such density that each is no more than the size of a city. A gamma ray burst expelled by their collision contains the energy of a billion billion suns which can last for a "long burst" of up to a hundred seconds, or, "short bursts," which last no more than a millisecond.

Once when I was real thirsty I had to stop at the only diner in town that worked. The whole parking lot was covered with crickets so by the time I crunched my way to the front door and smelled the steaks and the A-1 that'd be poured over that meat rushing out the air-conditioner vents I figured I'd had a journey on what planet I wasn't exactly sure but sure as shit every time I remembered that glass of water I'd hear every one of those crickets I'd crushed for it and wonder what kind of town Blythe was what the wives thought of the men who made them live in a place where the local crickets surrounded the restaurants and made the simplest night out into unbearable auditions that the women could hold far into themselves and wonder about who drinks and sinks them. So I'd try Needles even if crickets were there too. At least I'd go through Baghdad, not the one with Kish and Tikrit nibbling at its enchantments but the one between Klondike and Amboy, pass by the badlands of granite and lava surrounding Bristol

Lake where no soil development's taken place since the Hadrocyons, the dog-bears of the Pliocene sniffed the uranium shores of the Chuck Wallas.

Tuesday May 17th 2005: New proposals for changing the California Youth Authority reforms. The problem is the culture of violence that has been instituted for at least twenty-five to thirty years without the barest presence of rehabilitative procedures or programs. Rather the preference is the costs to keep each juvenile person in maximum control, isolation, reprisal and dysfunction and to spread the dysfunction into the costs per pupil per year in the school systems. A new study finds high rates of preschool expulsion of children in California: 7 per 100,000 expelled for behavior problems. The highest rate is for Black children. The study, entitled "Pre-kindergartners Left Behind" conducted by the Yale Child Study Center focused on 52 state funded pre-school programs. Such findings, though continuously shocking are and remain commensurate with the larger facts about the feeder systems in this country for its prisons and the allowable force of neglect at this earliest staging for launch.

California's average funding for pre-school students is approximately $31,000 per pupil per year.

For K through 12 students: $6,000 per year.

Compare these numbers with juvenile detention costs for males per year: $145,000: for females: $145,000 per year to create an utterly broken, enraged child with a 90% chance of recidivism. If these costs are the acceptable norm then how can the Guards' union go on claiming that the new programs in Missouri, Colorado and other states which are beginning to emphasize rehabilitative approaches after the historical disasters of their own systems, say such possibilities may not be "well suited to California's juvenile population" which Mike Jimenez, president of the California Correctional Peace Officers Association, called "older and more violent."

Jimenez also addressed what he called the larger, unanswered question: how any "new" programs can be implemented without raising taxes. The proposals have to this point no pliable, pragmatic details and the union which claims to endorse the "therapeutic approaches" doubts, at the same time, that any of "it would become reality" (the new estimated costs for incarcerating California's 1500 juvenile prisoners for the year 2009: $378 million or $252,000.00 per year per child for basic security and punishment).

> The zenith passage of the sun
> that day concerned World Failure
> and its symptoms:
>
> the "mining" of enemy populations
> for shrunken heads –
> the bones of the captives to be worn
> as regalia elaborately sewn
> into thick cotton warskirts
>
> whose emblems are monstrous flowers,
> the ritual pools where they floated
> meant to be tranquilly inviting
> surfaces of strangulation

a final ecstasy administered by those priestesses
whose specialties were herbs meant to mask such murder
as a calendrical number resembling the sexual visage of mountains
inhabiting the outer shades of the inscriptions the "and it
came to pass,
it was finished"   frozen in mid-collapse.

Sabrina Harmon of Abu Ghraib has been convicted of 6 of 7 charges. She, along with Charles Graner and Lynndie England, posed with the bodies of "detainees" – Ms. Harmon grinned for the camera next to a dead prisoner and was also pictured with another "detainee" on whose leg she had written "rapeist."

One of the surfers headed for this place called Laos said he'd gone in for a beer, heard this girl. Said she was really fuckin good, her voice and piano trailed in his ears all the way into those jungled mountains where some folks he wasn't supposed to ever name he said trained him to be a kind of werewolf top secret and all that kind'a shit you don't ever wanna whisper into the panties a' ini'a'yer friends so one night we opened the injectors of a blown "283" and went. And I mean this girl could twist the ranchers' sons and their lady friends from Rabbit Springs to Homer where all the poets can stumble west to Goffs and Fenner or east to Java where the desert becoming a shadow dancer's been known to give the blind sight that lies always just a little beyond description. Her music put her and us at least a thousand steps away from where our world started hanging either by its thread or some of the earliest reports of American rains so black and sulfurous that it was said those drops could be used for ink, to write about what deeper apparitions no one knows.

Friday May 27th 2005: A week of various ceremonials and closures. Graduation, introductions to parents and families, readying final thesis. And the "university"?
A body which seems so unsure of where it might belong or, if it does belong anywhere near its former identities. SDSU invited the CEO of a major South Asian conglomerate to give the graduating address to its College of Arts and Letters. The "firm" has its tentacles in fertilizers,

agribusiness, real-estate, banking, oil, and gold and in the spring of 2005 when many of these students feel themselves to be in a bewildered personal loss of ground, edgy despair about their futures, their senses of reality gone thinner every day, this "university" which now has new innovative majors in "Homeland Security" and "Casino Management" began its invocation with an introductory declaration offered by a dean for this visitor which sounded like an annual report to stockholders – then the introduction of the "speaker," not it turns out, the CEO himself, but the dude's son who could barely speak English appearing in his five or six thousand dollar black silk suit and begins his message with a tale of corporate improvements involving chickens. Ten years ago it took one person to "supervise" 10,000 chickens. But with the latest productivity improvements it now takes one person to "supervise" 150,000 chickens. This along with an historical outline of the father's corporation met with incomprehension, silence, aimless murmuring. A portrait of the turn-of-the-century university full of squalid distortion that either money can buy or the hunger for donations which forces the unknowing students, to, at the beginning of their adulthoods, swim in the same sewer as the institution which grants their degrees. The latest rituals of cynicism, cruel hypocrisy on the part of sickening adults and as the avian flu pandemic begins to emerge one can only wonder whether one of the "serviced" chickens mentioned in this graduating address will be the bird out of whose body the virus makes the species jump inframing the message of "improvements" delivered to this generation.

This day thankfully offset by students I've worked with who treated Gail and I to generous dinners with their families and, in one instance the following day, an extraordinary Hoopa Feast and Recognition Ceremony given by a family who came from the isolated Trinity River region of Northern California, to witness the accomplishments of my student, Cutcha. Food, song, and stories, and her father, a Hoopa Elder, made me a wonderful necklace – dentalium and beads tied in special ritual knots so that "Cutcha" (Bluejay) and I will always have a connection. Very moving and refreshing and something so thankfully lasting.

Saturday May 29th 2005: We walked around Lake Murray and had two lovely bird sightings. One, a hummingbird hovering over my right shoulder, examined me carefully then flew to its nest in an adjacent jacaranda tree. The nest no larger than my thumb and finely woven with various grasses and down feathers, the whole of the fertility labor appeared as beautiful basketry, keenly crafted reminding us of the Miwok and Yokut masterworks. Directly afterward we saw a yearling red-tailed hawk rise up from a clump of high weeds, circle over us at no more than twenty feet. It floated up to a eucalyptus branch where it preened and watched us, puffed out its chest feathers – a feast of wonders. And cleaning our yard this same weekend, weeding, trimming, we uncovered an alligator lizard, a rare species guarding her eggs under a pile of rotting palm leaves we'd months earlier cut down. The moisture and temperature of the decay obviously holding the conditions of birth. The five eggs were elliptically shaped, pink hued, about the size of a thin finger tip, and the mother refused to move from her protective hoverings and the call of her ancient heritage. She had lost her tail from some previous encounter and we, realizing our intrusion, immediately and gingerly re-covered the nest hoping somehow nothing has been overtly damaged or altered.

Miocene marine fossils have for decades been excavated in Orange County, California. This treasure of materials is the result of real estate development which has uncovered an extraordinary dimension of previous worlds, the most extensive collection of its kind revealing a record of life when Southern California lay under an ocean. One can visit the Orange County Warehouse and Historical Commission to examine these relics.

In many California prisons Criminon International has become a key player for "educational resources." Criminon is the "secular arm" of the Church of Scientology which has been allowed into Corcoran prison. The officials of the facility have lied about their knowledge of Criminon's presence. One of the main promoters is Gary Goddard, director of the prison's "educational services" who sought to create an illusion that Criminon has been officially sanctioned. Goddard wrote memos to supervisors praising the group, and in a June 20th 2004 note to the Warden, A.K. Scribner, claimed Criminon "has a long history of successes in the rehabilitation of inmates on an international scale." Here is a primary example of the collapse. Rather than "education" whatever that term had once meant, we now have "educational directors" in the prisons using their positions to promote organizations such as Scientology and making claims of international successes which are a menace and will place more lives and communities at risk. Schemes of infiltration like this, the attempt to use prisoners' lives as promotion is an inflaming barbarity, stealthy, netherworldly, morbidly ready to transform the brokenness into an even purer mineral. The fact of this sanction by men like Gary Goddard and organizations like Criminon indicate what may and can happen on the "outside" and bring us to an even starker threshold when one further considers U.S. District Court Judge Laurence K. Karlton who ten years ago ordered state prisons to improve their care of mentally ill inmates. He was alarmed at that time by reports of repeated failures in care at sites such as Corcoran. Judge Karlton is presiding over a 1990 class action suit challenging the quality of mental health care in the state prison system where 20% of the 171,000 prisoners in California are diagnosed with some form of mental illness. In one cell block, it was reported, inmates were confused, naked and without mattresses or blankets. In addition staff responses to inmates who failed to take medication was "irate" – "some renegade elements of custody staff apparently took it upon themselves to apply their own beknighted versions of how best to handle seriously mentally disordered inmates." Renegade guards and renegade organizations such as Criminon malignantly enshrine these lacerations on the Inside while on the Outside we watch the symptoms expand: since 9/11 the United States in the invaded countries has taken over 68,000 "suspects" into custody. The word which comes to mind, *Primitivbauweise* is Himmler's vocabulary rising up as a glassy-massed crushed zone of excited states in what we have embraced. The velocity of hate greater than the velocity of light. Qualitative temperature profiles available upon request.

Tuesday May 31 2005: Spent a quiet day gardening, gesturing toward new works. Late afternoon took out gnarled, knotted, twisted oleander stump with my chain saw, the one used to clear our house site in Shandaken. The plant is a powerful, regenerative being. After sunset we searched the night sky; saw Mars, Saturn, Jupiter, the Dipper very prominent. North Star vivid. A small but ugly report, Dick Cheney says he's "offended" by Amnesty International's critique of the Guantanamo Bay "detentions": "Frankly I was offended by it. For Amnesty International to suggest that somehow the United States is a violator of human rights. I frankly just don't take that seriously." What are the unrelenting implications here? Nothing frenzied, no lunging after excuses, explanations, nor fury. But rather the stark, sterile, guarded contempt, the mortar of vicious rottenness, impervious, closed up in its smallest volutions in order to birth the cruelties of its Virgin Babylons: "the vapours of the yawning pit" "heaps of smoking ruins" risen in the "Nights of American prosperities" and its "lulling cadences" of exculpation, turpitude, wily depravity. Blake's "blank in Nature" and in his geography "the cliffs of the Dead" infected with the "Science of Wrath."

"Where can a daughter in her water breaking live?" his mother would whisper over her clothes to be washed. Food to be cooked.

Monday June 6th 2005: Curious weather, rain last night, intermittent clouds which expand and then in their disappearance form a shredded complex expanding and darkening light. Today is "D-Day" – 61 years ago the young men of my father's and mother's generation walked into the slaughter which has never ended.

We went to Oceanside yesterday. Walked the pier. Some of the streets. The sad prominence of "Marines" – some back from Iraq looking tense and ravaged. Others – the about-to-go who will return sickened like theses brothers who vacantly smoke, spit continuously into the spaces around them. War surpluses on every corner, hookers subtle and not so subtle on side streets and alleys, girls attached to some dilapidated version of starlet magazine beauty hoping to marry one of the many scared never again to be normal boys or to roll'em for a day, a week, a month; the girls hard, focused, edgy as the boys sit in the endless barber shops getting sheared, coffin ready spic n'span. "Armies of the Night" howling in the shadows of the prolific stupors of this Age.

This city forbidding as the old Fort, where the Indians, the French, the peltry in beaver mixed with lead laced brandy in a coma sucking at the waves of desertions rimming the about to be coldly treasured future. He didn't know if his father had been conceived before or after the old grandfather'd got bit on the balls by that spider with its weird red hourglass to show its victims a last grain of sand spilled beyond any rescue. Was his father first generation after the visit of an eight legged girl who weaved her legends about the life of worlds and where they'd end up huge sexually for one night to be alive?

Wednesday June 8th 2005: Walked around Lake Murray earlier this morning. Sightings of osprey, mallard, pelican, nesting hummingbirds, lizards. The flora so fulminous during the earlier winter rains has dried up. We also had the skirts of our palm trees cut away. The palms had become a haven for rats; so that's done. Gail doing initial bisque firings in her electric kiln – preparing to do glaze studies and experiments.

Saturday June 11th 2005: Another heavy blanket of mist last night. Today, late morning, still cool, overcast. Yesterday at the San Diego Museum of Art. A show entitled "2000 Years of Latin American Portraiture." The emphasis was primarily the colonial experience but the show began with small magnificent Maya and Mochica faces. The quality of the Mochica "stirrup" head pieces always astounds. Much of the European based eighteenth and nineteenth century works were stiff, deadened, clumsy but there are instances of illumined care; portraits by artists "unknown" which dug into the paint with some unhesitant discovery. Two pictures of young women were very compelling and two portraits of the dead lying in "state" – one of a child and another, a young beautiful nun. The artists in this case specialized in this form of portraiture obviously in a hurry so the brushwork has about it a freshness an airiness even before the Catholic morbidities mixing with the ancient trance intensities of Mexico. The poses Aztec-like but the Christian layers of repellence smooth and secretive and Jesus stunk in their full, cold, savageries. There was a David Siqueiros painting which Gail pointed out, was much in its handling like Alice Neel.

Benjamin Paul has died. The student of Margaret Mead's and the founder of "Medical Anthropology." A brave man who did much of his work in the Guatemalan highland town of San Pedro La Laguna. When the plague of "Disappearances" began once more in the late 1980s Paul co-wrote with William J. Demarest "The Operation of a Death Squad in San Pedro La Laguna." His great piece, "Health, Culture, and Community: Case Studies of Public Reactions to Health Programs" examined how traditional communities struggled to accept health innovations and suggested that international aid programs would be more effective if they considered local cultural beliefs. In San Pedro La Laguna church bells tolled after residents heard about the "curious and talkative professor with the mischievous smile." The town's first secondary school, named after Paul and his wife, was built on the land they donated.

Monday June 13th 2005: A crisp breeze, our windchimes at song. Yesterday began with an earthquake! 8:30am, the house jolted, Gail in bed reading said the bed "jumped" as if moved by an invisible animal which seems most appropo for what that description might hold. Heard reports of swaying telephone poles, buildings rumbling (as did our house). The epicenter for the quake: Anza California on the Riverside/San Diego County borders, a 5.6 Richter Scale measurement. No injuries. We spent the afternoon planting vegetables, putting up trellises – the vegetable garden has a feeling of emergent resource, beautifully crafted as Gail designs it and makes it come true. Very exciting especially as one tries to envision "urban" gardening and spaces on a smaller scale, the renewing shapeliness of one's own private possibilities.

The girls. They weren't from the beach. Their bodies weren't primed like a backyard bullet or some missile in a silo filling its birthhole with flames, all that speed equipment pumping for the biggest inch of death. Their make-up drooping in the early summer heat, tits sweated up, smashing the mosquitoes that'd been in that air since old Queen Anne's skeleton glimmered with furs.

Watching the insurance industry as it attempts to insure even greater war profits in Iraq. Has the blood price ever been so completely unmasked, the negating specialized malignancies of these materialisms attempting to polish an end to time. And where do Hardy's great saddened passages from "Tess of the D'Urbervilles" possibly fit?:

> Day at length broke in the sky. When it had been day aloft for some little while, it became day in the wood.
>
> Directly the assuring and prosaic light of the world's active hours had grown strong, she crept from under her hillock of leaves and looked around boldly. Then she perceived what had been going on to disturb her. The plantation wherein she had taken shelter ran down at this spot into a peak, which ended it hitherward, outside the hedge being arable ground. Under the trees several pheasants lay about, their rich plumage dabbled with blood; some were dead, some feebly twitching a wing, some staring up at the sky, some pulsating quickly, some contorted, some stretched out – all of them writhing in agony except the fortunate ones whose tortures had ended during the night by the inability of nature to bear more.
>
> Tess guessed at once the meaning of this. The birds had been driven down into this corner the day before by some shooting party; and while those that had dropped dead under the shot or had died before nightfall had been searched for and carried off, many badly wounded birds had escaped and hidden themselves away or risen among the thick boughs, where they had maintained their position till they grew weaker with loss of blood in the night-time, when they had fallen one by one as she had heard them.

The activity done by the most "civil persons" as the author places it who "... made it their purpose to destroy life ..." And for the Person, "Tess" of the novel, the first hints of the catastrophe "a new strange sound among the leaves" "a sort of gasp or gurgle" that couldn't readily be identified. Hardy has, in this, a new concentration on the skillfully slow, withering currencies of human distraction and his questions in 1891 and their burdens extend to these early 21st century moments; the pressures of the violences appearing with such delicate strain in the novelist's landscapes which by their mercilessness evoke the delectations of plutocracy that needs slaughter, the new mysticisms of our 21st century private game preserves/plantations which are the equivalent to "Space Luxuriencies" – think of this for instance in relationship to "Virgin Galactic" out of Mohave California. Virgin Galactic is already in the process of marketing 2.5 hour flights into space for $250,000.00. The company boasts it will offer " . . . an . . . experience unlike any available to mankind . . . for the first time in the history of the universe . . ." Bookings began in 2005 and "Virgin" has five nearly space ready prototypes and will, by 2008, be ready to launch all five ships everyday from its Space Port America site in New Mexico. "Virgin's" Space Port will feature a new "Luxury Experience" with hotel space both on planet and off. Each ship will have the capacity for five tourists apiece and once in orbit the tourist will have five minutes of luxury experience before re-entry trajectory begins. Remember, in this, 1968 when, after the first extraterrestrial touchdown by "mankind," Pan Am booked over 100,000 tourists flights to the moon even as Vietnam had been transformed into "The Slab." One thinks of incorporation before these ancient numbers out of that American year, the marketing cycles and their energies of antagonism a modern personality needs spreading new fatalities and fatalism no one seems to recognize nor wants to name or the lies that personality needs to incorporate in order to live and by which the individual achieves her or his renunciation of the foundations of reality as Theodore Adorno examines the phenomena in "Minima Moralia." But for myself as a novelist the phrasings in Hardy's sentence "When it had been day aloft for some little while, it became day in the wood" hold the barely emergent pulses of the unruffled calms to come which are the prerequisites of the perfected horrors, the plantations of land mines planted so carefully by hand and the spells of this handwork, this enrooting. Is Hardy's achievement, to enphrase De Kooning, a way of painting and by that reconfigure what the painter said so long ago about being "wrapped in the melodrama of vulgarity" and its condition of undistorted wanderings Hardy's sentence awakens? The strange gurgling sounds of the civilization in these throes as if the Body Politic not only of the United States but the World has become an inchoate shadow eating, disfiguring, rising from the twisted alchemies of the Jornada del Muerto and the "Trinity" – poltergeists of the Jesus Hungers slurping the perils and agonies of World Injury, feeling nothing before their frenzies and desecrations and the sly morphologies rendering as nuisance and dead the word "Humanity" its old, charmed vindictive free meanings merely appendages cast aside for the more serious species "Zero Option" with its Aryan embrace of optimisms and leering inter-planetary utopias.

Tuesday June 14th 2005: still overcast with interspersed afternoon sun. Concentrating on summer chores: painting and sanding inside doors, outside porch pillars, and window frames. The Supreme Court overturned two murder convictions in Texas and California. The convictions were poisoned by prosecutorial racial biases instructing that jury selection exclude African Americans. There is a 1963 Dallas "prosecutor's manual" that warns, "Do not take Jews, Negroes, Dagos, Mexicans, or a member of any minority race on a jury no matter how rich or well educated." These attitudes still prevailed up to the time in 1986 when Thomas Miller-El was tried. There is evidence that prosecutors questioned potential Black jurors more aggressively and shuffled the seating of the jury pool in hopes of moving Whites to the front. The one Black juror accepted was a strong proponent of the death penalty. Justice David Souter said the jury selection process was "infected" by racial bias. He described as "trickery" the prosecution's use of different questions for White and Black jurors and he dismissed the "incredible explanation" for why certain Black jurors were excluded (prosecutors said they excluded the potential Black jurors because they were leery of imposing a death sentence).

The U.S. Senate issued an "Apology" for its inaction on the terrible lynchings that took place in the United States from 1890 through the 1930s. This "Body" acknowledged " . . . that although 200 lynching bills were introduced only three passed." The House and seven U.S. presidents lobbied for such laws. None was ever approved by the Senate. Each time the House passed an anti-lynching bill, Southern senators filibustered them – once in a monumental battle carried out on the Senate floor for six weeks in the 1930s.

Who can degrade the faintness
the indifferences
teething in the throat
planted as wild teeth there

Wednesday June 15th 2005: 11:00am, overcast. Walked around Lake Murray this morning hoping the hummingbird we saw last year will come back to her nest. The lake is low but still there are egrets, red-wing black birds, jackrabbits, ground squirrels, and spectacularly beautiful flowering datura. More revelations today. The Bush administration planned to initiate the war long before 9/11. The democracy in its present state shows not the barest spasm, barest revulsion toward these leaders, each the "Polypus" of Blake's narrative risen from the Web of Death woven in Cathedron's Loom. No Human Form, as that Bard says of these creaturely types, but only fibrous vegetations.

"Loud sport the dancers in the dance of death rejoicing in the carnage"
A new state prison site has just opened: Kern Valley State Prison.

The cost for design and construction:	$397 million
Annual operating costs:	$136 million
Workforce:	780
Support Staff:	365

Inmate Capacity: 5,000
Total land needed: 600 acres (one square mile)
Kern Valley is ex-governor Grey Davis's last contribution to the Correctional Officers' Union)

June 16th 2005: the Bolivian Revolution is rising up in resistance to Bechtel and Haliburton who want ownership of the Sky and the Rain: " ... in what eternal, unstirring paralysis, and deadly hopeless trance ..." says Melville of life insurance companies whose mining processes are similarly oriented to the modern corporation's application of the supernatural agency of guarantee. At no time in our previous histories have we seen an attempt to claim ownership of the Sky Rain and Water as the corporate "person" begins to assume larger impersonations that have been lying in wait.
More Guantanamo ulcerations. Senator Jeff Sessions of Alabama proclaimed yesterday, "This country is not abusing prisoners. We have no policy to do so. And it's wrong to suggest that. And it puts our soldiers at risk who are in this battle because we sent them there. Some of the detainees need to be executed." How is one to sound the pathology of this language. Are these the symptoms of parasitism and its accompanying morbidities, a fear of Biblical leprosy induced by a sermon heard in childhood and manifesting itself in this form of violent twisted speech, or is this language an exhibit of a decay process and its possible relation to "AaA," the ancient Egyptian name for disease causing forces and these primordially joined vowels designating the desperate mummification of certain fish? (as I re-read and edit theses passages today, July 30, 2006, the Egyptian vowels seem to enwreath and suffocatorily expand: the Bush administration will be "opening" a new state-of-the-art maximun security prison site at Guantanamo: a $30 million two storey jail built by Haliburton and, apparently, modeled on a jail facility in Lenawee County, Michigan, another rural American locality that has been able to avoid economic collapse through the prisonboom).

Did Edgar Ray Killen say the same thing to his fellow klansmen as Jeff Sessions said about "Detainees" in 1964 before Michael Schwerner, Andrew Goodman, and James Chaney were beaten and shot?

Here yet another "senator" from the Deep South calling for murder out of what traditions of lynching, burning, mutilation rising up out of the Protestantisms that cannot seem to function without the grotesque brooding meanness of hysterical racism no matter what its masks.

Is the most telling deformation of the war the massive food shortages plaguing the Occupied under the Spreader of Democracy?

Saturday June 18th 2005: 72 degrees, sunny, a beautiful wash of morning desert light, a dry breeze, and our cactus flowers variously appearing.

The rulers are altering documents to favor cattle ranching on public lands. The Bush administration violated critical portions of a scientific analysis of the environmental impact of cattle on public lands before announcing Thursday (June 16th 2006) that it would relax regulations limiting grazing on these lands, according to scientists involved in these studies. A government biologist and hydrologist who both retired this year from the Bureau of Land Management said their conclusions that the proposed new rules might adversely affect water quality and wild life, including endangered species were excised and replaced with language justifying less stringent regulations favored by cattle ranchers.

How is one to examine the hero cult of the mutilators. Coleridge in his "Lecture 6" addressed the issue of "property":

> Inequality originated in the institution of landed Property – In the early ages of the World the right of landed Property must have been none or transient – a man was proprietor of the Land only while his Flocks were feeding on it . . . As Manufactures improved and the artificial Wants of Life increased, inequality of Life became more mark'd and enviable and the motives to mutual Injury numerous.

From their undisciplined Passions as Individuals and as Communities, private Vices and public Wars became frequent – and the
influence of Kings and Chieftains increased with Despotism. Thus
the jarring Interests of Individuals rendered Governments necessary and governments have operated like quack Medicines; they
have produced new diseases, and only checked the old ones – and
the evils which they check, they perpetuate ... Since the Revolution
(The Glorious Revolution of 1688 under the reign of King James II)
we have been engaged in perpetual Wars – in the course of which
it has been calculated that more than ten million Lives have been
lost – Yet for no one of these Wars could any cause be assigned
which would have justified the Death of one Individual – they every
one have originated in the Folly and 'Prejudices of our Monarchs
and the wretched compliance of Ministers, and through them we
are a bloodstained People ... What, that can deprave the understanding and subvert the integrity of the People, does it (the government) not employ? It has spread among us almost an universal
contagion of depravity – the Minister is bribed by his Offices, the
Senator by the Minister – the corporation Elector by the Senator,
and the citizen by the corporation elector – Selfishness is planted
in every bosom, and prepares us for Slavery which it introduces.
There is scarcely a Vice which Government does not teach us –
criminal prodigality and an unholy Splendor surrounds it – disregard of solemn Promises marks its conduct – and more than half the
business of Ministers is to find inducements to Perjury! Nay of late
it has become the fashion to keep wicked and needy men in regular
Pay, who without scruple take the most awful oaths in order to gain
the confidence which it is their Trade to betray ..."

The last sentence of the quote is Coleridge's reference to the "system of
Spies and Informers" his government hired to infiltrate the private world
of citizens; activities which the Poet felt initiated a "deprivation of private

morals" and destroyed the bonds that make any society possible, Love and Trust. The gentle Coleridge making his fierce Examination.

Our friend Flame took us in the morning to the Griffith Park Zoo which turned out to be very special. The animals were active and curious. The zoo was filled with kids running from one astonishing creature to another in their awed wonders. We saw a new-born tapir as well as a South American "Mane-Wolf," a long legged rare species, graceful, curious, extremely shy. Saw a huge mandrill baboon and remembered at that moment L.S.B. Leakey's uncovering of fossil gorilla sized baboons in the Olduvai Gorge; species which lived alongside Hominid ancestral forms. Afterwards Flame gave us a "tour" of LA's East Side with all of its geographies of Latin America. Every neighborhood aburst with its own living sounds and dreams in this cauldron of experiments that is the Border Region.

In the afternoon we drove to Long Beach where I did a reading from "Prisons: Inside the New America . . ." The bookstore called "2000 and One Books" is owned by a Black couple who have over the last thirteen years made their store into a community and cultural nexus. We were stunned. I went for a nervous pee, came back and the place was packed. People came from all over LA and the reading turned into a "Town Meeting"; intense, moving – Black Vietnam war veterans with their wives – people frightened by what has happened to their civic world.

Friday June 26th 2005: Sunny, a slight breeze. Yesterday did jury duty; sat for seven hours, not called, so I guess my name will appear in the lottery next year.

Edgar Ray Killen, the Ku Klux Klansman who incited others and planned the killing of Andrew Goodman, James E. Chaney, and Michael H. Schwerner has been given a 60 year sentence for the murders. "Justice" whatever it is, is late (41 years), but at least this man along with Sam Bowers, the

"Imperial Wizard" who instructed Killen to organize the killing party, will go to a hell not even the Bible can comprehend. What do I mean by "hell"; the Keepers who are aerosol ready, sensor alert, no-spall maintained, germicidally delivered: transforms the Bible, Creation, Imagination, Art, Health, Desire, and Nature into domoic whirlpools and makes those domoic whirlpools acceptable alternatives to Being. But here the unfortunate question does rise up: are we immersed in the symptoms of a new slavery, the slavery to domoic disintegration, self made, self inflicted, born of our own civilization? And if so, what new Abolitions must we begin to Imagine?

Alberto Gonzales wants continued "flexibility" in setting more stringent prison sentences imposed by Federal judges. More cement for the gravestones of this America conjoined to the "Product Defense Industry" which specializes in the "manufacture of doubt" "uncertainty" toward the issues of climate and planetary health, the making of the world's continental shelves into neurotoxic puddles. The buyers? The tobacco Industry and Corporations. "For fifty years," writes David Michaels in an editorial commentary today in the LA Times, "cigarette manufacturers employed a stable of scientists willing to assert (sometimes under oath) that there was no conclusive evidence that cigarettes cause lung cancer, or that nicotine is addictive. An official at Brown & Williamson, a cigarette maker now owned by R.J. Reynolds, once noted in a memo: 'Doubt is our product since it is the best means of competing with the body of facts that exists in the mind of general public . . . ' It is now unusual for the science behind a public health or environmental regulation not to be challenged. In recent years corporations have mounted campaigns to question studies documenting the adverse health effects of exposure to, among others, beryllium, lead, mercury, vinyl, chloride, chromium, benzene, benzidine, and nickel . . ." Buy a lie, a lie that mangles, disfigures, and kills torturously via cancer, slow suffocation, inch-by-inch cell-by-cell deterioration.

What exactly is the real "oil strike"?

More and more it seems the source is "Udan Adan" Blake's "Ocean of Death Sweat" and who are the new Columbuses and crews?

I think of Artaud's piece "On Balinese Theatre" and his phrase "under the sign of hallucination and fear . . ." and the uprising question at the beginning of Chapter XIX "The Prophet" in "Moby Dick" having to do with who signs on to what ship and the articles of the contract: "Anything down there about your souls?"

Saturday June 25th 2005: The Battle of the Little Big Horn; 129 years ago. Custer was another tyranos wanting and demanding the sacrifices of his soldiers as he strove for a possible "presidency" but ended up rotting himself under the boiling sun of that terrible American afternoon.

The people we were fighting. They knew how to shoot. Head shots that would come from nowhere and left you inside this shame for being there to see it and smell it. It couldn't be filled up with anything. Nothing. No one could prepare you for what it felt like to see a man that way. I didn't want to say too much about that, its perversion. The things it'd make me ask and wonder. Get me or someone else churned into a run through the fuckin procedures. He said he didn't want me to live to come back thirsty for a surgical noose, swell my veins like so many others where we came from. And here was the ochre. If it made them come alive in the world of the dead then maybe it'd do something for me. *The shadows underneath. They were filled with tunnels and boys uniformed and masked. Their steps throbbing against secret stairs. The greasy infected cement, cracking with the strain above it, its surface ready to erupt downward into this place. In one corner, a couple there is locked in a candle lit dance. The woman's hunger.*
She wants the male to unwrap himself. Show his penis. When she sees it a sound from her throat equally blood chambered rushes over the masked boys in the semi-darkness wanting someone to kill. Her teeth have the sexual carnivals of her past etched into them. Her laughter animates the held scenes and the candle formed shadows on the walls behind them flutter with the growing erection, its transparency

meeting the facial dangle of her tongue, the sleeve of her labia lushly flowered. On one of her teeth dawn has the jaws of water without flesh. The direction of the journey shines there.

Monday June 27th 2005: We worked this past weekend; sanding and stripping doors, painting and preparing our den for Jim Christiansen's craftsmanship.

A week of political séances, Senate majority leader, Bill Frist, a medical doctor, tried to deny he made a video diagnosis of Teri Shavo's "state" even though the episode was recorded. No suppleness. Only flagrance, calm, steadfast in its debasements.

Dick Cheney backed away from his statement:

"The insurgency is on its last legs."

These words a tangle of ennobled malice let loose as "politics" have now become our common writhings and mutual hostilities. Cheney's statement may arise from the sureties of mass arrests and the pens to hold the clientele. Thus the information about the expansion of prisons in Iraq and Camp Bucca near the Kuwati border. The army is also working on the construction of a third major prison near Sulaymaniya – there is also Ft. Suse, a former Russian-built barracks near Sulaymaniya. "Part of it used to be a prison, so it should be easy to renovate," said General William Brandenburg, the "overseer" of U.S. run prisons in Iraq. "Renovation" reformed as a Corrections specific verb with a washfast garment horizon, a full line purity stream offering minimal chains of inconvenience. And the adverb "easy" in-framing this American general's attitude toward the transformation of the "space" that surrounds him; "ease" dropping out of its Old French and Latin parachutes notifying ourselves yet once more how comfortably we have enjoined ourselves to the long term durability characteristics of our domestic and foreign "justice facilities." And if the army is central deliverer of "product" there how long will it be before the Rumsfeld/Bush new army is central deliverer of "product" here?

Number of prisoners now in Iraq: 10,178
Number of prisoners awaiting "processing"   1,630

In California the costs for keeping aged, ill prisoners has no apparent ceiling.

The number of men and women over the age of 55
in the system: 6,400
The number of second and third strikers who are destined
To grow old and die in the system: 42, 240

Hundreds of these prisoners already cost the state over $400,000 a year a piece for health care. J.P. Trembly, an aid to Correction Czar, Roderick Hickman, stated, "We believe if people commit a crime and have been tried, judged, and sentenced, they need to serve the time. Just because we're in a budget crisis we can't make crime and punishment decisions based on fiscal concerns." A budgetless system of retribution – the once twice whatever it takes long-term solution mystical affordable lightweight transportable scheduled for corrections delivery on any asteroid or pre-oxygenated planet in-waiting. The diphthongs of "need" tied to the vowels of "serve" whether from Middle English, the Latin, or Etruscan origins the pop-up noun is still "slave." Fanny Howe says in "The Wedding Dress" "The prison system manipulates the people it incarcerates in order to see if they can be deformed and become something unrecognizable." But if the experiment has become a "Criminal Justice Studio" of design principles, service provisions, and nationwide office locations providing assistance to local associate firms then the "something unrecognizable" is part of the new, more helpful arsenal to meet increased demands for service.

Sex mummy come to bathe everyone in something huger than any Egypt ever was or could be, say Charlton Heston, climbing down from that phosphorous laced weed like a miracle mile Moses with those petroglyphs, says the ostrich feather, says.

Wednesday June 29th 2005: The great historian, Shelby Foote, has died. He wrote his pieces on the Civil War under a picture of Marcel Proust, working from 9 to 5 on what he considered personally homely labors.

The Bush administration, in the midst of this war, has produced a billion dollar shortfall for funds to cover the health care of veterans. Along with this shortfall senate republicans have consistently voted down all proposals to enlarge VA healthcare programs.

Are the maimed and violated to be considered too cost heavy, and, if they are still useful, fodder for the prisons either on planet or off?

Some got it from spiders, arms swelling like stuffed inner tubes; human extremity become a raw flange, the mind connected to it wondering about its own body's combination, and whether after the ten thousand choices of antigens it might try to stop the arachnid proteins with, it'd quit, say fuck it, you can have this one I'm riding. Let those packages of DNA go squirt their goddamned ways into the future on my own indifferent venom time sway with a vindictiveness that could kiss you back to the Eocene when these death touchers with fangs and poisons to put the brain down or rot the blood appear along with the giant horse-gulping birds that wandered the savannahs of North and South America for nearly fifty million years and you can finally walk real slow figuring someone's business is really older than yours no matter what war hole you crawl down and get jaw fatigue from what you eat there which includes that deep freeze delirium sending you a paycheck burst from the sniperman.

Friday July 1ˢᵗ 2005: Foggy and cool earlier when we went for our six mile walk around Lake Murray with "Iris" who has become a fine dog. Saw two blue herons. They seemed to be in some sort of combat; fierce cries and squawks, poses, and then a chase along the watery edges.

Judge Thelton Henderson has placed California's prison health-care system under federal receivership. The judge said that he was especially alarmed by the uncontested statistic provided by a court appointed expert "that a prisoner needlessly dies once a week" due to a collapse of basic care in the system. An attorney for the inmate plaintiffs claimed in a 2001 class action lawsuit that the prison health care system of California amounted to unconstitutionally cruel and unusual punishment. The court experts found few signs of progress toward any improvement and provided chilling examples illustrating filthy conditions, ill-trained and neglectful doctors and a pattern of preventable deaths that one expert called "macabre" and unlike anything" he had ever seen before. The "expert" in this case is Dr. Michael Puisis, author of "Clinical Practice in Correctional Medicine": Correctional Medicine across the nation is a contract for profit bonanza led by such companies as "Prison Health" and "Correctional Medical Services." The specialty of these contractors: lethal cost cuts and the hiring of doctors and nurses with questionable credentials for a treasure of billions. Does such neglect amount to a culture of execution without sanction and designating what hemorrhage at the hidden unadmitted core of our lives? This American version of the SS, killing by novel non-invasive mutilation pathologies, or, call it "A note on Dispeopling First Interplanetary Settlements: Concerning Earlier Defects of Organization."

Bernie Ebbers wants out. Though he stole $11 billion he desires to surrender his remaining fortune of $45 million for the court's mercy and to avoid dying in prison. No one has been able to re-define the depth of these "white collar" criminals and their crimes which are violent, compulsive acts of savagery and permanent mutilation that force us all into realms of heartless shadow play.

Saturday July 2nd 2005: The U.S. Senate has agreed to revive the "Bunker Buster Program." Linton Brooks, head of the National Nuclear Security Administration, and Donald Rumsfeld insist "the country needs to develop a nuclear warhead that would be capable of destroying deeply buried targets." Such a weapon "could cause from several thousand to one million casualties, depending on its yield and location," Brooks acknowledged, and further stated, "There is no way to avoid significant fallout of radio-active debris from such use . . ."

> Sprout Name of Time
> suck out the names
> who will peck the plague dry

If you walked out into the forests surrounding the City on the Straits anytime from its foundation to the early 1840s before those primeval stands had had their bark circled one tree at a time over millions of acres you could have found under that canopy raspberries, whortleberries, cran-berries and strawberries, the ancient abundance nearly as lovely a gift as the shade and dappled light which had called it to unfold as soon as the ice of another world had gone stagnant.

There were so many different kinds of shade to choose from that the unde-cided pilgrim could dance herself helpless for at least three lifetimes over a hesitation about which maples to sit under, what walnuts to pick. Getting too comfortable under your favorite oak might be a hazard because down the meadow directly there'd be either a plum or wild apple tree and the urge for one or the other before that snooze set in could destroy the science of laziness you were about to truly degrade yourself with in front of the sky loads of feather borne meat come to flit over your dreaming body and then go roost for free in the butternut and elm. With your reveries taking place on a rise above Lake St. Claire you'd have been able to look down on that water and the huge shadows its schools of fish made. Pike, Bass, Sturgeon, Pickeral, Bullhead, Perch, White Fish, Trout migrated from one fresh water sea to another forming underwater clouds that would have seemed to contain no end. Moose, Bear, Buffalo, Elk, Deer, those shoals of fresh water ocean fish, and storms of Passenger Pigeons were the meat supply for a least a thousand generations.

Tuesday July 5th 2005: Worked on our house; painting, sanding, peeling old paint off with a heat gun – projects that have been waiting. Last night went to the Rothenberg's for a 4th of July banquet which warmed our hearts – we even sang "America the Beautiful" reclaiming our country from "California to the New York Island."

The LA Times had an editorial this morning focused on the Bush administration's re-writing, editing, deletions of vital scientific and environmental studies some of which amount to more than criminal violation. The White House, for instance, in 2002 barred the release of a report that found levels of mercury in women of child bearing age are high enough to damage unborn children. The report was finally released after an Environmental Protection Agency official leaked it. The spokespersons for "The Rights of the Unborn" revealed in their truest labors of protecting the Poisoners of the Unborn as an acceptable rate of statistical birth deformity in order to insure continued prosperity. How can one ever resolve one's feelings toward a civilization that would use such sickness to service its own gains and call to this ghost horde as the source of fevered moralities while at the same time covertly allowing brain death to drip into the wombs of its female populations. The function here is to poison both women and children and to enslave them in moral intoxications to Molech's delight. Both Blake and Ginsberg with their lovely and tender intelligences have made this into one of the central themes of their poetry exposing that form of extremity where all other joys in becoming so distant and displaced that the only delight left is cruelty. And is this realm "a veil of soul making" as Keats declared in the fullness and generosity of his humanity?

Wednesday July 6th 2005: A cool wind and so far a cool summer. We're at our labors, restoring doors, tiling, taring roofs.

Read a Paul Krugman editorial in the New York Times about the "Center for Consumer Freedoms" website. This advocacy outfit for Coca Cola, Tyson Foods, and, among many others, Wendys, states: "Far too few Americans remember that the Founding Fathers, authors of modern liberty, greatly enjoyed food and drink . . . Now it seems that food liberty – just one of the many areas of personal choice fought for by original American patriots – is constantly under attack . . ."

"Food Liberty"?

What could this bizarre "liberty" be and are we discussing the "right" to be obese and has the whole thing collapsed into what Lawrence called "our eunuch civilization" with its "sneaking, sterilizing cruelty"?

Thursday July 7th 2005: Awful news from London. Four separate bombings. People killed and injured. Daily life sunk in horror and pain. The bombings took place in the King's Cross section of central London exactly where we lived and walked and took the Tube. We've written friends in the UK. Everyone thankfully OK but weary, worried.

Beans climbed their cornstalks, pumpkin and squash strung as far as the eye could gauge. A chaotic, random planting meant reduced soil loss and more work for insects who, because of that, couldn't destroy a human concentration on one yield only. Prolonged rigorous apprenticeship equally awaited the hunter who had to know down to the most obscure detail the behavior of the animals and himself. His stamina, eyesight, threshold of pain, the physical and mental condition of the hunted, size, age, the insects that came to bite them, season, lay of the land and who else out in the nothingness was also hungry, human and non-human, pursuit, butchery, preservation of meat demanded the total resources of body and mind. You could do everything perfect and still end up blinking over how a last kernel of corn might get fifteen men, women, and children over that six weeks hump before the bursts of new life appeared.

Robert Scheer wrote an op-ed piece today – Karl Rove and the Valerie Plame scandal. Mr. Scheer, at least, is finally using a vocabulary which visits the facts. In the end, though, what Rove's leak (we know now in April of 2006 that it is Bush's leak) and Novak's column really exposed was the depravity of the administration's use of a false WMD threat and its willingness to go after anyone willing to express the most woefully shrunken truth.

Summer seems to have arrived except for the late afternoon fog banks similar to those of Marin County.
A Terrible Day
Four Al Qaeda operatives have escaped from the Bagram prison in Afghanistan. This facility a major segment of the Bagram Air Base head-quarters for US military operations in this now even more tragic country. The blending of our power and stupidity seems the nearly perfect mixture by which to sink into these seething ancient canny worlds we have invaded and which have already swallowed us without our knowing exactly in what ways we have been devoured.

What about her lovers? The ones she allowed at the edges of her feminin-
ity to make her labia swell, hold their breasts and nipples to the breakages
of hot breath between her upper and lower teeth set to bite the equally
womanly flesh above or below her? Her own womanhood erect splitting
the protective shield of lips folded in the precisions of flesh to be slipped.

The last of a series of Pentagon inquiries in to the "detainee abuse"
begun after the Abu Ghraib revelations is now officially "closed." The
"conclusion" of this final investigation "closes the book on the Pentagon's
examination of detainee abuse worldwide." In the instance of this inquiry
"Military investigators recommended that the former commander of the
US military prison at Guantanamo Bay, Major General Jeffrey D. Miller
… be reprimanded for his role in detainee mistreatment at the facility, but
a top Army general rejected the conclusion . . ." The reprimand was
rejected by Army General Bantz J. Craddock, Chief of the US Southern
Command in Miami, which also oversees operations at this prison site in
Cuba. The investigators determined that the interrogation techniques
used on Mohammed Al-Qahtani, a "high value" prisoner (the "20th high-
jacker") did not "rise to the level of inhumane treatment" though the techniques used "were degrading and abusive." Craddock rejected these
findings of Lieutenant General Randall N. Schmidt and Brigadere
General John T. Furlow "on the grounds that Miller did not violate US
Law or policy."
Our rulers have finalized the legitimacy of the "quaint" in relationship to
the Geneva Convention. The conjunction of our domestic prison industry
and our world-wide dentention/renditions represent the certainties of disintegration merging with a new generation of plutonium 238. Is there a
difference between this "production" and the final set of "inquiries" into
"detainee abuse" on a world-wide basis from Guantanamo to the secret
pens on our warships to the Black Sites of Eastern Europe, the Middle
East or the other on-planet asteroidal destinations? This is where senator

John Warner's 2004 vow to fully reveal the truths of Abu Ghraib dribble away and become a part of the fantastic paradoxes only Goyas's "Tooth Hunting" might explain in Los Caprichos.

Thursday July 14th 2005: A cool wind, overcast, humid. Heard Borrego Springs reached 117 degrees.

Amidst the tragedy of yesterday's information about the official shut-down of inquiries into our world-wide prison industrial complex and the abuse of detainees come the findings of a report entitled "The State of Black Los Angeles" by the Urban League and the United Way of Greater Los Angeles.

This report appears 40 years after the horrifying Watts Riots, the urban conflagration which initiated the complex, bitter racial horrors of the 1960s. The data is its own macabre sorrow indicating that though some high income Black households have increased, that a high of Black children have health insurance (94%), and 63% of Black children attend pre-school along with the fact that African Americans have increased representation among the City's top elected officials, the majority live in the words of the "Report" in "sickness."

1. Blacks are twice as likely as other groups to be the victims of violent crimes.
2. Death rates from homicide and HIV/AIDS are more than three times higher than other racial groups.
3. More Blacks receive public assistance and more Blacks live in poverty.
4. Blacks have arrest rates far higher than other groups.
5. The LAPD searches Black and Latino drivers four times more often than Whites or Asians but only 38% of Blacks are found to be carrying illegal firearms compared with 55% of Whites, 65% of Latinos, and 54% of Asians.

But the most damaging problems remain unchanged over the past 40 year period.

Blacks have the lowest median household income:	$31,905.00
Latinos:	$33,820.00
Asians:	$47,631.00
Whites:	$53,978.00

Blacks though 10% of the population make up 30% of the homeless.
56% of the hate crimes are committed against Blacks.
44% of Black high school students fail to graduate within the required four-year period.
Home Loans: 5% for Blacks. Whites who make up 31% of the population are given 72% of all such loans.
The premature death rate among Blacks in 40.6 per 100,000. This number far exceeds the rate for Latinos at 11 per 100,000. For Whites: 4.5 per 100,000. For Asians: 3.8 per 100,000.
The premature death rate for Black teenagers is 131.4 per 100,000, a number that astonished even those who compiled the materials for this report.

In 2004 19.8% of Black drivers were stopped by the police.
Whites: 12.6%
Latinos: 11.2%
Asians: 10.1%
The national average for Blacks is 12.3% yet law enforcement officials deny they practice "racial profiling."

32% of Black males born in Los Angeles in the year 2001 are likely to go to prison in their lifetime. For Latinos the number is 17%. For Whites the number is 6%.

These numbers have a chilling similarity to the findings compiled in 2004 which I cited in "Prisons: Inside the New America from Vernooykill Creek to Abu Ghraib": A Black male born in America in the year 2001 has a 1 in 3 chance of being imprisoned in his lifetime. Can such statistics be included in the smoking ruins of the World Trade Towers and the collapse into the fathomless morbid drift of our barbaric remove? The number which may more accurately evoke the sordidness of that remove defines the expansion of nuclear blast wave, equally our own invention, and what happens to the air we breath when subject to the equation:

$$Pr=2p \frac{7po + 4}{7po + P}$$

Who is to say, given these statistics, who is living in "sickness"?

Thursday July 21st 2005: The monsoons are upon us with remarkable variation. Yesterday at 2:30 pm the temperature gauge registered 103 degrees. We thought the beach for a late afternoon would be a remedy but the immediate coast-line was covered in dark thick storm clouds and at least a 35 degree reduction in temperature along with rain showers and soaking winds pushed far inland.

New reports from London about 3 attempted bombings which thankfully in this case were not successful but horribly frightening and sad. This information juxtaposed with a report on mid-western "water parks" indoor recreation facilities which are open all year round (90 to 100,000 square feet). The piece was accompanied by an interview with a developer who used these adjectives to describe one of the "parks":

Huge
Wonderful
Monstrous

Saturday July 23rd 68 degrees at 9am a 35 degree drop from yesterday's temperatures. For the last two days the weather has been summer-like — clear skies, hot, windless. Now it's overcast and last night a heavy sky churning thunder passed over this coastal desert city.

He'd go down to the fall runs then alone, do the curls none but the best surfers'd try who watched him from those beaches as they waxed their boards and thought three or four times about heading out into those waters that could take a body the way top most skies of an earth take noiseless meteors. The hours spent making his body into that knife slicing the whole weight of planetary ocean, seeming to strip it back letter by letter to a namelessness again, and maybe learn how to live there not going forward backward but invent what could be braced out of the half shreds in the final letter.

Tuesday July 27th 2005: Hot summer in full. Jim Christiansen came yesterday to install the last of our new energy saving windows.
"Military dog handlers at the notorious Abu Ghraib prison engaged in a competition to see which one could make inmates defecate and urinate on themselves."
A riot took place at the US compound in Bagram Afghanistan. Eight people were taken from a village and "detained." The crowd protesting the arrests shouted "Die America." And what would happen to us if a billion people were to concentrate on this phrase in mass unison, calmly begin to shout these words and not stop shouting these words?

And if the ancient forest still inhabited the unmoved core of this world whether a city had been erected there or not then you could go down any of its alleys or broken streets wavering in their ends where the fingers of the dead dance on the palms of the living where women in their hunger for fish become snakes and disappear forever into the dream instructions their men cannot ever hear where the crows cry "How did I come to be alive?" "Why am I in this world?" "Where am I going?" and then eat the youngest children of mankind first where the sister lurks who fixes deer-shit soups where spit from the cannibal brother can bring back the disappeared twin of the body where ancient grandmothers can drink whole lakes where bowls wait filled with magical vomit where a woman's flayed skin hangs unbearably singing where the chestnut roots and the seven sisters murder beneath it near the edges of the rising sun where moles swallow men into their journeys where the big as a cloud butterfly brings dying and sicknesses every other day where the uncle has eyelids hanging to his cheeks where moccasins wait made of a woman's labia where dice made of the owl's eyes burst with their seeing.

Ginsberg on O'Hara: "He was at the center of an extraordinary poetic era . . . which gives his poetry its sense of historic monumentality . . . And he integrated purely personal life into the high art of composition, marking the return of all authority back to the person. His style is actually in line with the tradition that begins with Independence and runs through Thoreau and Whitman, here composed in metropolitan space age architecture environment. He taught me to really see New York for the first time, by making the giant style of Midtown his intimate cocktail environment. It's like having Catullus change your view of the Forum in Rome . . ."

Saturday July 30th 2005: Spent the afternoon yesterday body surfing and watching our young friend, a professional surfer, catch his waves. He is a spectacular craftsman who sets himself into a motion of body control unlike anyone we've seen. Not a frenetic surfing style biting into the waves with the choppy motions of a one winged wasp which can be a fascinating frenzy, but a kind of pelican grace, gliding in solitary man-weight as his ancient counterparts glide in their bird-weight an inch above the peculiar immense indifferent face of sea rhythms at this shore.

Today we heard something we could have never anticipated – the radio roars of the planet Saturn as recorded by the Casini Probe. A planetary sound so startling one is left in the wonders over one's own breath before the vibratory darknesses of these melodies and the conjunction of this "contact" with all that presently envelops the fate of our own Planet/Life as one regards the sickened Saturnian violences which now accompany our daily life and these leaders as Saturnine monstrocities sullen cold steady in their compulsion their spite and what Frank O'Hara would have seen as the signs indicating that these people totally regret life and would force the rest of us into the reign of that regret and its images – a "Not of this World" as the older stories might place it. A reign where there are only corpses left and a single dwarf who offers to show the emperor of these results the lifeless world which has come to pass. I am also reminded of Robert Creeley's projection of a time when there will be only ourselves as saddest company having at some increasingly now comprehensible point erased every other creature. And are we in some sterilized upsurging conjunction with the first landings of the "Pilgrims" who found whole villages curiously intact except for the piles of skeletons where those people in their last moments of stunned anguish clung to each other as flies from offshore European ships orbited and dropped their payloads?

Oh Excellent Demon bring your new tumors mutilations your car bombs cereals fence monitors ova of ancient parasites your stand up to daily life abuse-proof laminates your air-born mercury floating over Vegas your more advanced surface bursts

Saturn Giver of the Measures of the Cosmos
Babylonian Star of Law and Justice
Egyptian Star of Nemisis Ruler of Necessity and Retribution
Star of Amnesties

Renewer of Health lessening the hold of Revenge and Brutality – the Golden Age of that Time when one knew neither war nor bloody sacrifices And Dinosaurs. The oldest embryos so far discovered were found in 1978 underneath the 183 million year old Drakenberg lava outburst in South Africa. The eggs had to wait for the present technologies (miniature jack hammers and drills for use under more powerful electron microscopes) to remove surrounding rock. The findings reveal the possibility that the newly hatched infants were surprisingly helpless and required intense care from parents.

She knew some of the stories too from the Indian women she'd loved. There were ashes of females somewhere still in those forests that could give birth to the men no bigger than the hole in your tooth but none of those lovers ever told her how old they got to be and whether in their growing they end up in the farthest regions of the sunsets calling to the Who's Around to Hear. Those women told her what not to do at night, the noises and whistles riding unsuspectedly underbreath which attracted ghosts or even the Facelessness of the World calling all of the missing parts of Itself in to a sudden ruptured completeness. They'd whisper about exiles in Florida swamps or the marches of the starving, touch her breasts with certain feathers they'd never name and in the morning knead pan-fried bread for her with honey because she'd been their lover for one night. She couldn't reconcile the way a word and the breath made out of it seemed to split apart when most men spoke and how women heard and felt the actual dissection, knew the unaccountable weddings between the unreal and the word towers it attracted larger than any life's preparation, or at least the life she held. "Maenadic" she'd heard of that. Women among themselves, yearning, their concentration spoiling the wives for men who would increase the rule of labyrinth, every portion of it tied in Hera's knots. Herakleotic Knots her lovers told her about, the epidemic of rape agony and its arrival on the land and how the daughters in some now unreachable time sold themselves off into madness because of a mass suicide of the mothers. These incomplete maps of a haunted persecution. Women in bars, the ones just traveling through who stayed in hidden valleys of northern Greece or Turkey, whispered in bed to her. Their hatred of labyrinth and narrative the map of retributions against those who eat the savior scorn the genesis of souls stained with the necessity to tame the danger in women. The story choked at either end. Sons and husbands forcing their ravishments down the generations – mothers daughters mistresses of the labyrinth and the Age of Honey darkened by their flight from the feminine sphere punishable by death. The girls would swing from trees to honor the mothers' suicides the fullness of women among themselves the hanged and their epidemic. The persecution of women for their rage and in the background the nurses of a new mind a new world executed en mass for their attentions. A blood bath. A sea of women's blood marking the agents and their catastrophe. Thetis in her water breaking as the voices of the story gather. Realm of the dead opening for what is most alive. Thyiades, the mature women. Their pilgrimage to renew existence their voices and frenzied dances enter no literature no art. Yet they swarmed in their trances over winter deadened mountains frost bite licking at the protective seal of ecstasy. Their "white feet" their menace awakening sorrow no distance can keep enacting the whole community of Life stolen. Mere women's actions and lives dissolved, the ripeness of males entrusted to them for endless birth. Who would not fear it?

2003NB3R3: A new planet discovered in the Kuiper Belt larger than Pluto.
70% Rock
30% Water Ice

Minus 400 degrees Fahrenheit even as the US Department of Justice released its first statistical report on prison rape and abuse acknowledging that much of the sexual violence in prisons was (is?) probably never reported. This "Other" planet and the report which accompanies its warning that there is and never was any reliable estimation of the unreported sexual victimization of its population. The 2004 estimates for incidents of rape of the persons on this sphere are 8, 210 (is this number similar to the Number 30 in relationship to the Iraq War; all civilian casualties up to the number 30 in any bombing or combat incident do not need scrutiny or report – anything above the number 30 as estimate needs to be signed off by an "official" – the further question: where did this number come from before the acknowledged underestimates of over 100,000 civilian deaths?) in a national jail system that holds over 2 million people. This is the adult statistic. In the state run juvenile facilities on a nation-wide basis allegations of staff sexual misconduct ran proportionally almost 10 times higher than for adult facilities. No one any longer knows whether 2003NB3R3 or Earth is the colder planet as America "spreads."

Begin with an examination of strawberries then expand into the ancient forest gardens on the shores of the fresh water seas where women specializing in baked corn dumplings, fried grasshoppers, walked every inch of huge peach orchards, their botany and its scale producing over a million bushels of corn a year, fields hoed and weeded for miles outside a village and the interspersed adjacent woods reserved for beans squash and the griefs that could send a captured enemy into a roasted shred murmuring over the Rim Being at the end of worlds and the Begging Heads come to visit and take final possession of the lost before another garden poised at that moment in 1725 when in Paris there appeared men and a female to be exact: an Osage, a single Chicago Chief, the ambassador from the Metchegamais, one Oto, and one girl from the Missouris. It is reported they were beautifully formed, their bodies enhanced by scars, tattoos, sweat gleamed paint to make the air of that Paris seethe with a curled reckless-ness of the wild glamour, their headdresses and robes a ceremony for the hottest dreams to accompany the marriage festivals for the King, Louis XV, and were they like quail slipping through some other grass, an ocean of it conspiring exotically to be these suggestions hovering at the roots of a Detroit or a San Bernardino with its mission graveyards the names there left out of the real estate mythologies and what is a mythology now other than a service provider to sell MacMansions or MacPrisons sprung instantly onto any land or seascape anywhere?

An interview with a Space Shuttle female crew member speaking with George Bush: "We believe in getting off the planet" – A new dimension of "faith" in planetary abandonment for whom? And are these final more fantastic depravations such as the American mining operations of Freeport-McMoRan in New Guinea and the Canadian Goldstrike Mine in Elko Nevada, two of the largest gold mining sites on the planet, pro-found examples of the hurry up method of total environmental disin-tegration designed to enhance such off-planet beliefs with a presence of collapse so final, so splendidly malevolent that either mourning or sorrow become the merest costumes before this statement of joy and its release from what these trace elements of futurity already see as a worn-out world to be picked apart in these last centuries of patient refined savagery.

Get me a chopper with the money. If I lived. I didn't feel like I knew where I was until I saw the blimp hangers and sugar beet fields above Costa Mesa. Lead tinged smogs mixed with the smells of burnt sage euca-lyptus wild live oak a little whistful taste of burnt fibre glass roof shingles. Those smokes serving me up a platter I'd just left; shit and napalm boiled landscapes. One segment of a planet and the poor bastards on it flying in compound reverse toward the Galactic Lords of Intestines to be digested outside the reach of any humanity.

"WE BELIEVE IN GETTING OFF THE PLANET" Are the reservoirs of Mesopotamian fossil oceans the haruspicies of a planetary abandonment propaganda? asks the haruspex pouring oil on water. Bird Keeper who watches the severed wind pipes of eagles and the God voices held there. No "e n" priests alive now to read the old omen collections with any helpful precision. A question for the God who burrows and curls in the still fresh raptor viscera:

    Does the Iraq War have anything to do with the state of Bush's liver?

    Answer: Yes

    Question: Should we look to malformations of the Sea?

    Question: What malformations?

    Problem posed: Would the mortal answer break the heart of the ancient being?

    Of the Next Query:

               Look to the Summa a lu

    Question: What group of omens?

    Answer: As to the Flight of Whales: Tablets 57 through 63

    Question: And if they have turned to dust?

    Answer: Refer to the Death of Frogs in the Older Sequences of the Malformed

    Question: Are you referring to the lost names of Demons?

    No Answer:

    Question: And where will there be well-being when women and men and their children at last learn to scorn it. And if the dreams, the old dreams of lion- headed eagles return, what then?

Answer: Look yonder to a sky of wolf eating sparrows.

Question: And the Death Pit at Ur. Did the Girls sing themselves to death there and has their song at last reached us?

Answer: Never and twice.

End of Query of the Eagle's Windpipe

The accumulation at La Brea began about thirty-six thousand years ago. But teeth will tell a story almost no other part of the body or perhaps even the mind itself can bear given the implications of strangeness that may have started there and then leaked out all over everything. What narrative the extinct can tell might only attend shadows but shadows glow too with the mistrusts of a dispossessed blankness. The jaws of the fossil predators trapped in these asphalt seeps may contain a signature with a long, unwelcome endurance. This colonial Rancho unlike most sites is a house of carnivore teeth where at least ten meat eaters were called to their ends by each stuck and sinking herbivore. Smilodons, coyotes, dire wolves, and American lions suffered a frequency of broken teeth on these shores nearly five times the rate of their modern carnivore cousins. The majority who lost their lives here approximately ten thousand years ago exhibited only slight tooth wear and were young adults in their prime, not the injured or worn out. I want to ask some ifs working on me; if their broken teeth are a ripple bound to our unnamed hungers carried from the coasts of these miniature Pleistocene death oceans? If the map of their wreckage was swelling and who'd be the poor son-of-a-bitch to hear its nearnesses before anyone else? I remember when I started asking these things. Went to Laos as a volunteer murderer all the way to the Plain of Jars and stared into those giant two thousand and more year old urns. Nobody still knows who carved out that sandstone or why they left them there from horizon to horizon on the Xieng Kouang Plateau. Maybe those people left them to hold the true invisible spillage of what they knew to be the time to come, saw a residual glint of the unappeared future and not knowing anything else to do with that clairvoyance, went to work on these vessels. May be too they were womb corridors and from there the severed heads of my ancestor Olmecs flew in a sky to the jungles of another world daring all the human noise that ever was or will be with their immovable sexy lips. Staring into the opening of one of those jars finally became not much different than staring at the popped eyes of a "bird stone" the faraway Red Ochre People made on the coasts where Lake Michigan in its southern bulge juts into the tributaries of the Falcon Dancers who carried their severed heads from the plains of Illinois to the meadows of farthest Alabama.

Friday August 5th 2005: Two pieces today about the prisons. Steve Kruse, warden at the Stockton Youth Correctional Facility site, on May 27th of this year used unreasonable force against a juvenile ward handcuffed but struggling. Kruse grabbed the 19 year old by the hair and jaw and slammed the ward's head into a wall. The further aggravation: neither Kruse nor any of the prison staff who were present reported the incident, thus maintaining the absolute code of silence which drowns all detail in this abyss. A violent out of control warden in a state operated juvenile facility demonstrating the fact that handcuffed shackled children are still the easiest pickups.

The other: Maribel Cuevas of Fresno; an 11 year old girl who, after being baited and taunted by a boy with water balloons and rocks, picked up a stone herself and threw it at her tormentor. The result: a head gash. Two children in an ugly tussle which should never have reached a further level of response except the local police and district attorney's office created a cause and attempted to make an example of this girl. The police arrested her on suspicion of felony assault. She spent five days in Juvenile Hall, then was placed under house arrest and forced to wear a monitoring anklet for 30 days. The young girl was deeply frightened and traumatized but the police and mayor stood by their official behaviors and stance. Fortunately there were responses from around the world which led to her probation. Maribel Cuevas was very lucky. The two incidents exemplify how far we've journeyed toward the butcher's hook manufactured by William Bennett and John J. Dilulio's Jr.'s claim that we are endangered by a horde of super-criminal children. Here is an American community frozen in terror over an 11 year old girl ready to impose either its Biblical Wrath or Expert Violation under the cover of policy and the use of reasonable force.

August 6th 2005: The Bombs were dropped on Hiroshima and Nagasaki 60 years ago.

August 9th through August 29th: Visited Clay and Sarah in New York. Saw Gail's mother for the last time in final stages of Alzheimer's Disease. Ora, rather than becoming paranoid, bitter, and twistedly angered which could certainly have happened, became angelically quiet and watchful and floated in a decreasing set of responses as if her mind were a pond under a sun shrinking in its circle; no rain, no shade sitting out her days and nights her lovely greeting smiles bearing no form of recognition. Her whole person come to some distant, fragile, bewildering kindness as dear Gail searched for spoons her mother could more easily hold growing as she did less and less able to find her mouth in the act of simple eating.

Tuesday August 30th 2005: 8:50am, 87 degrees. Watered the front yard and shopped for basics. Coming home to our small pleasures; the vegetables and fruit trees are ripening. Our salads are delicious. Gail's concentration on direct foods without the deluge of carbohydrates is beautifully satisfying as we return to these delights and waitings.

John Bolton has introduced a major sabotage of the UN's studies and nego-
ciations calling for extensive reform and "world action against injustice,
poverty, and environmental catastrophe" as the LA Times editorial states.
"His most odious change was to delete all references to the Millennium
Development Goals which commit the advanced industrialized nations to
cut world poverty in half by 2015." The "Have countries, would, under
the terms of this agreement, eventually have contributed 0.7% of their
gross national product to foreign aid" as a recognition that all people have
the right to be free from misery, starvation, and preventable disease and
that those able to pay have some responsibility to alleviate needless suffering. Rimbaud's country gentleman of a bleak land dedicated to torment
and the "certain convivialities" of dread.

Very good news. Our dear Clay just got into a new program at the School
of Visual Arts initiated by Thomas McEvilley; very exciting.
The media is filled with terrible images of Hurricane Katrina which seems
to draw at least ⅓ of the Caribbean into its maelstrom and which has now
devastated most of the "Deep South." New Orleans 80% flooded. The
Mississippi, Louisiana, and Alabama coasts ripped to shreds in the largest
"natural disaster" ever to plague the nation.

Goddamned condors, Peregrine warriors. And the beast giants who sweep
the sky of this earth every fifty thousand years with their spider webbed
mouths; cities, oceans squirming in the filaments. We drove to LA. Talked
mostly about the Salt Flats at Bonneville. Racing. How those sodium pans
might be the best place to squirt yourself right out of sea level time at
three to six hundred miles per hour. And the piston wizards we knew who
could modify the metal into a rent-a-special space-time bullet, manage
proof your regrets into the other gulped out evaporations hammering at
the edges of this inland sea since the ground sloths and camels grazed at

its shores. Engine shops with blowers and injectors hovered, ready to be dropped over manifolds, exhaust header ribs and pop-riveted streamliners tunnel tested down to the last aerodynamic blister, the slippery side of five hundred miles per hour wrapped in air density and horsepower. Get up past six hundred and you could start seeing the smoke signals of the Anasazi transform the Cricket Mountains into mirrors.

The six youth facility guards who beat juvenile inmates one year ago have been rehired and as Gloria Romero says, this is a setback for efforts to improve the system and represents a point of cynicism and the absolute inability to want either to recognize the disrepair and its long-term consequences or to do anything else other than solidify profits from it. Each of us sailors, as Melville might say, gladly being sold "deliriums and death . . ." Whose voice will clean our world as Frank O'Hara said of Boris Pasternak in "Memorial Day 1950" Cold War and of the men who made us, they "hollering like stuck pigs" at the edge of being they are about to initiate.

Thursday September 1st 2005: A fascinating piece today; the genetic blueprint comparing ourselves with chimpanzees. The differences between species are "a mere sliver of DNA." The actual changes amount to 200,000 of the 3 billion chemical letters that make up the human genome occurring over the 6 million year horizon which separates the forms. Researchers also identified six regions where genetic mutations appear to have spread rapidly throughout human populations in the last 200,000 years. One of the regions contains the gene FOXP2, which is associated with speech development in humans. These sudden changes or "Selective Sweep" has made humans susceptible to cancer, Alzheimer's Disease, malaria, AIDS, and other afflictions which do not occur in Chimps.
"The overwhelming similarity of the human and chimp genomes, and the incremental nature of the changes that set them on different developmental

paths, validate the mechanics of evolution." Though the Theory of Evolution is under attack by the proponents of intelligent design, Dr. Francis S. Collens, Director of the National Human Genome Research Institute observed he could not think of a better way to prove the Theory "short of a time machine." The scientists found that evolution was more flexible and in some ways simpler than many had previously thought. Dr. Christopher A. Walsh, a neurology professor at Harvard Medical School, said the studies "showed that a small number of changes were enough, demonstrating the power of evolution to respond to circumstances." Researchers, however, still don't understand the significance of the "Selective Sweep" nor "FOXP2" in terms of how it functions in other mammals and ourselves.

Could such information increase the invitation for living and being rather than withering the invitation and how are we to hear Cheney's call for a more "robust executive" and the various precursor forms of "Robustus" haunting his language and its suggestion for a more athletic tyranny?

Friday September 2nd 2005: Joseph Rotblat has died at 96. Hero and founder of the Pugwash Conference and the only scientist to resign from the Manhattan Project in horror over the use of atomic and nuclear weapons. Both he and Bertrand Russell appealed to Albert Einstein to lend his voice to the cause of nuclear disarmament, resulting in the "Russell/ Einstein Manifesto" which declared that atomic weapons "threaten the continued existence of Mankind." His great vision was to eradicate the need for military confrontation which seems the next phase of evolutionary "Selective Sweep"; if we can keep ourselves intact long enough for the evolutionary angel to touch the species DNA.

Long rides in the desert had made it so. A five hundred mile drive was a step practically to the back yard, even a kind of habit, to talk over a case of easy beer eighty miles per hour at the moonless juncture where the Mojave becomes the Sonora and the geologic debris past the shot-gun window are chunks of Venus went on a hundred million year goof and slammed into the strontium veils where raw houses arrive enframed in the even rawer landscape, subdivisions cutting in where there had never been water and never would be and in this fringe world the most elemental greed to've ever got hatched, the one for liquid mixed with real estate myth footed in the earlier soul hungers of the padres that make of the Gold Rush even Tlaloc's double-serpented terror face look like a chain of nothin more than earthquake mutilated ten cent stores gone along for the two hundred seventy million years it's taken for the planetary neighborhood to spin once around the galaxy.

And a picture of a white policeman holding an M16 on a busload full of New Orleans "evacuees" who are all Black. The tone of the image – a prison bus straight from corrections central. Add to this Bush's incredible statement this morning about Trent Lot's loss of an expensive home in Biloxi and how he, the president, couldn't wait to sit on the senator's fully restored front porch once more. The "decider's" speech was slurred, uncomprehending. He appeared to be so sated with rest and sleep and quarantine and health, and 15% body fat ratio so trampled and revealed and drooped in his lethargy that that effort at merest gibberish recalls the most curious fracture of syllable Chapter XV ("Chowder") in Melville's book " . . . I. A Coffin . . ." heavy with hydrocephaly mind flood and where an "I" or an "A" might form in the count of vowels as if Katrina herself were some species of sea monster "touching the plain facts, historical and otherwise of the fishery . . ."

Sunday September 4th 2005: What are these American Days? I think of Frank O'Hara's "Meditations in an Emergency" and the fiercely tender lines there about any of us as American Beings, our experience, the "mysterious vacancy" and before its travail

> " . . . to keep the filth of life, away, yes
> there, even in the heart, where the filth is pumped in and slanders
> and pollutes and determines . . ." in the "greenhouse" that is ours
> and no one else's.

Emily Metzgar of the Shreveport Times wrote an essay today about the long-term corruption of Louisiana's government and its traditional lack of interest toward its neediest residents. "The state's indigent defender program is in desperate need of reform, but change is being blocked by powerful political players with vested interest in maintaining the system as it is. The high school drop-out rate – already tied for worst in the nation – is rising despite much touted accountability efforts that still fail to keep kids in school. The per-capita prison incarceration rate is the highest in the country without the accompanying high rates of crime . . . Kids Count, the annual ranking of child well-being, ranks Louisiana 49th for its overall performance, and no wonder. Nearly 50% of the state's children live in poverty (as do 15% of its residents over 65). In New Orleans, the Census Bureau reported that 27.9% of the population lives in poverty-more than double the national average . . ."
Along with this flood of numbers consider that fact that 65% of White Americans do not believe that racial discrimination exists and 75% of Black Americans believe it does. The "appalling mists" to use Blake's terminology: the nectar and spell of our slumbers devouring the present and future health of what populations to come. Here also the too tidy thing we've made of Blake's "slime of ancient horrors" as our own versions of odor of deceit, vagueries of optimism mixing with labors, in the Bard's time as well as ours, of "law blasted wastes" weir speak grown enormous

as in the FBI's "Concern List" over Black Muslims in the prisons spawning potential Al Qaeda recruits. Out of the mining techniques of our "appalling mists" appears this latest paranoia and demonization of the already abandoned, the reduced. A body politic childish, fearful, constantly irritated with "ruins congenerated" found in the epic "Jerusalem" which whispers of tyrannnies.

Where can we begin to conceive of a new "Arete" as Robert Duncan proposes-an image of "Vital Living" apart from the threatening conclusions which surround us?

Sunday September 12th 2005: The portrait of John Roberts is of a man grooming his ambitions carefully and smartly. The Before and After Person of These Shadows. Roberts opposed Affirmative Action, protested an expansion of the Voting Rights Act, urged an end to "forced busing" for school desegregation, supported a move in congress to strip federal courts of jurisdiction over school prayer. As a lawyer for the first Bush he urged the Supreme Court to overthrow Roe vs. Wade. He also stated that inmates on death row were not entitled to a new hearing in federal court even if newly discovered evidence indicated the condemned were not guilty of their crime. He saw little use for the landmark Title IX Law that has given females equal rights in schools and colleges. The nominee also went to the Supreme Court where he argued that girls who were the victims of sexual abuse by teachers or coaches or school officials could not sue the schools for damages (the Court ruled unanimously against him).

Wednesday September 14th 2005: More than 14 of the Guantanamo "detainees" are on hunger strike. Many have vowed to die rather than continue to remain alive in the humiliation and shame even as John Roberts has recently ruled as a member of the District of Columbia Federal appeals Court to uphold Bush's creation of special military tribunals for alleged terrorists who will under these rulings be denied the protection of the Geneva Convention.

Tuesday September 20th 2005: 10:15am, 78 degrees. Thunder last night and some sprinkles. Sound of boiling sky.

Army Pfc., Lynndie England will abandon her earlier courtroom strategy and fight charges that she was a key participant in the abuses of detainees at Abu Ghraib. England is the last of the junior enlistees charged with abuses. The new defense: mental health problems that extend back to childhood. This, the young girl at the center of the homely pictures, unconfused, even amused as she cockily hovers in the cordialities of a cruelty that could have as easily appeared in the back pages of a high school year book – the lighthearted touch of the gruesome adjusting itself for the proper pose, the stagecraft suspended as of the bells of a datura waiting for hummingbird or bee smiling at the end of an over-dilated nonchalance.

Thursday September 22nd 2005: 42nd anniversary of JFK's assassination. 10:45am, 99 degrees. Autumn has arrived with its spell of heat and last night the Moon and Mars appeared as marvelous twins.

Saturday September 24th 2005: Abu Ghraib continues to be a geology that refuses to submerge. Army Captain Ian Fishback and two unnamed sergeants in frustration over the continued inaction of their superior officers contacted Human Rights Watch and senators from the Armed Services

Committee. Their allegations, if correct, represent the most serious episodes of prisoner/detainee mistreatment at Abu Ghraib:

> "... blows to the head, chest, legs, and stomach ... even deliberate breaking of bones ... pouring chemical substances on skin or eyes ... this happened every day ..."

One of the strangest theories of Ice Age extinctions so far to be introduced: super nova debris may have been responsible for the death of mammoths and other large fauna. If so, why not homo sapiens?

Tuesday September 27th 2005: Lynndie England has been convicted of six of seven charges in a military court marshal. Sad. Great sadness and mourning. And as Charles Olson said 1952 America in Cold War:

> "There is no hope – except in the living being who wants a difference, in short, in what he or she does with his or her own alive life. No knowledge of civilizations or present conditions is the equal of this conundrum ..."

How place these words before the malignancy of these images and this war which with each revelation brings to mind what Olson also earlier said of our participation as Americans willful or not:

> "of the most organized attack on the good which men, it does seem, have ever mounted ..."

This war and the prison industry which apart from all other government expenditures has been subject to no cost analysis. The projected price of the conflict:

1 to 2 trillion dollars

16,000 Americans injured (as of this date, January 11th 2006)

20% of these injuries are head wounds which will require either long-term or life-long care.

A young woman so deeply sure and secure in malformation. I think of Rimbaud's "Vies."

And is his address in the last lines to the "Living" of a future or to our specific selves less and less startled by our own suffocations:

"What is my nothingness to the stupor that awaits you?"

the Poet asks so dangerously showering whoever we might be in the calmly pleased maniacal lechery of these pictures and the population who scrambled and coaxed these appearances out of itself.

(A note. On Tuesday August 1st 2006 it was reported Maj. General Geoffrey D. Miller, the commandant of both Guantanamo and Abu Ghraib, hand selected by Rumsfeld and other pentagon players to "improve" interrogation techniques at both sites, has not only been allowed his full retirement, but has been awarded the Army's Distinguished Service Medal. If you do not believe prisons are a central triumph then regard General Miller's "Hero's Welcome" and consider, as well, Conrad's sentence at the beginning of the "Heart of Darkness": " . . . A taint of imbecile rapacity blew through it all like a whiff from some corpse . . .")

as if the earth under our feet
were
an excrement of some sky

and we degraded prisoners
destined
to hunger until we eat filth

while the imagination strains
after deer
going by fields of goldenrod in

the stifling heat of September
Somehow
it seems to destroy us

It is only in isolate flecks that
something
is given off

No one
to witness
and adjust, no one to drive the car

William Carlos Williams "Spring and All"

Friday September 30th 2005: Our coastal desert still under the charm of the Santa Anas. Dry hot winds scrubbed sky gone bone blue.
William Bennett, hero of conservative moralities, author of the "Book of Virtues" stated yesterday on his Salem Radio Network show, "But I do know that it's true that if you wanted to reduce crime, you could, if that were your sole purpose, you could abort every black baby in this country, and your crime rate would go down." The "eternal unstirring paralysis" to use Melville's words. And this business of perfecting wrongs. I think of William Bennett imagining the descent of George Washington into his soul for further authorship of "virtues" and of Melville's imagination of this same "Father" and "Fatherhood" itself under the strain of Christian unmoorings as in "A Bosom Friend" (Chapter X): "Queequeg was George Washington cannibalistically developed" and the cannibalism of this moralist's is it statement, observation, wish-projection? This force of charitable acknowledgement that the Black Unborn as opposed to the White Unborn, inconvenient as they are, can escape prison, can escape being the burden they are and are destined to be by present projection of numbers based upon present

trends of civil disintegration, that they, even in utero, are a Crime Rate. Is this what Lawrence was saying in "Studies In Classic American Literature" about "the whole Sermon on the Mount" becoming "a litany of white vice?"

Better to decorate yourself with sex and music and if you had hard feelins to lay'em up on a bar before they became the Death Valley summer dead mummifying to a trespass no explanation'll volunteer to cover. Say breath and being hearing and smell are vapors. Each of them trees waiting for the sap breathed from the Beforetime Others. The ancient women's discovery of intimacies, intelligences, moistures in their impressions. BreathSouls panted out in mindful wanderings. Drops of saffron for the clitoris in those twilight generations. Crocus. The stigma erect receiver of pollens dried to pungent aroma two and two in the swayings. Let its fragments go hard and dry into the seasons of women who gathered death in their baskets and there was still no knowing how far they had come and gone right under the eyes of a world which might always remain blind to them. The infection traveling. Fat thigh bones of she-goats, necklaces of wove flowerheads, dill shoots for curls, pink-ankled charms. "Hero" "Timas" "Anactoria" "Athis." All were of "beautiful dances" flowing in the immediacies of said speech on torn papyri destined for garbage and throats of mummified crocodiles. The rebellion waiting for another age like the water signs of the Shoshone, and the only thing to soak in those neighborhoods is dust of alkali where the children were fed bird tongues for wit and quickness.

Monday October 3rd 2005: Spent the afternoon at the Sea; full of marvels-washed up kelp and stone and millions of exposed sand clams, each one like a snow flake, no two alike in their remarkable colors. Water very warm and clean but surf so small and slow no throb to hold the body.

The destruction of the army is in accordance with the civilian leadership. "The army has decided to accept a greater number of recruits who score near the bottom of military aptitude tests." The administration's explanation for this is an astounding maze of further disorientation. The original standards ("They really weren't standards. They were just guidelines," said Army Secretary, Francis Harvey) were "established to prevent the military services from meeting recruit quotas by accepting too many people with low IQs . . ." In this mad twisted sales pitch are we sending our most heavily armed cretins to "spread democracy"?

"Democracy in America was never the same as Liberty in Europe. In Europe Liberty was a great life throb. But in America Democracy was always something anti-life. The greatest democrats, like Abraham Lincoln, had always a sacrificial, self-murdering note in their voices. American Democracy was a form of self-murder, always. Or of murdering somebody else."

This heaped up American phantasmagoria, phantoms to be let loose with their night gear over the Mesopotamian oilfirs and how harsh or misplaced is Lawrence's statement if one examines the "Black Sites" "Abu Ghraib" "Bangram" the grotesque of the democracy similar to the description of the Pequod under Peleg's chief mateship:

> "A cannibal craft, tricking herself forth in the chased bones of her enemies . . ."

Robert Duncan's observation in "Man's Fullfilment in Order and Strife" is also of use here (though this poet too despaired over "our manner of speech" as a "cover" for the ruthless wastes and pollutions which are the more livid and lasting guarantee of our freedoms: witness the "forever problems" of the present technological age – fiend tombs for the tons of plutonium wastes and our contemporary search for a "warning symbol" that might adequately speak to a projected 100,000 to 150,000 year future;

our present paranoias of Alert Theory crazed with images of cyborg feminist corporations poised in that "then" refusing to believe the ancient male warnings about to infect them and digging into the still potently fatal "Waste Isolation Pilot Plant" or WIPP salt caverns stuffed with the sludges of nuclear weapons production ready to wreck planets and galaxies – the cannibal tricks of our world and the drama of our deep sicknesses being played out in these scenarios of future murky feminism incapable of "reading" or "thinking" as the present players imagine it in their game scenarios of what to do with world-wide waste hazard sites).

"Blake looking into the beginning of the American Revolution saw the Revolution of the States as belonging to the drama of the deep sickness of Europe 'where the horrible darkness is impressed with the reflections of desire.' Blake's vision is of a confusion of intents and powers that strikes true to the confusion in which America was born. At first seeing Washington, Franklin, Paine as heroes rising in the flames of unfulfilled desire, rising to liberate Man from his bonds of repression, Blake came in his lifetime to see Washington as he saw Napoleon, as a 'heroic villains' for following the subsidence of the American and French Revolutions came no liberation of Man's nature from the external repressions of social law or the internal repressions of the super ego . . ."

Further, Duncan says, "The angel Albion appears in Blake's *America* 'a dragon form, clashing his scales'; and the shadowy Daughter of Urthona, 'Dark Virgin,' the suffering spirit of America, appears as the Bride enslaved addressing her groom:

> I know thee, I have found thee, & I will not let thee go.
> Thou art the image of God who dwells in the darkness of Africa,
> And thou art fall'n to give me life in regions of dark death . . .

Blake saw the soul of America as a shadowy bride whose black husband is in chains; or a black bride whose true groom is the enslaved spirit of

Europe hidden in Africa. The reality of our history appeared in flames and agony where a spiritual alchemy was at work to unite in marriage Heaven and Hell or the Righteous and the Damned . . ."

Blake in his prophetic rage also saw that rebellion against empire begets empire anew, Revolution condemned to age as an "Eternal Viper self-renew'd":

> Heavens; Eternal Viper self-renewed, rolling in clouds
> I see thee in thick clouds and darkness on America's shore
> Writhing in pangs of abhorred birth; red flames the crest rebellious
> And eyes of death . . .

The Poet recognized the future plagues of obedience and conformity surging up in America and Europe. He knew these were horrible visions of stern torments accompanied by the images of rulers "glowing with blood." Though I think this made him sometimes despair over the repugnant visionary burdens of his art's fullness he was still able to proclaim in the abyss of unutterable shambles and convulsions an aptitude for a more thorough archaic matrix of visionary stamina starkly uniting him to his personal devotions and that would not make him immune to cynicism (I don't know how that can be possible) but lessened the complicities between rage and cynicism that charges the Prophecies not with fulfillment but with the tricks of their impersonations making of the intelligences rage can hold a perishing invasion of the Polypus who lures each human creature passing before it into murdering its own soul with the sensuous afflictions of cruelty and contempt. Blake allowing himself to be caught in the Loom of these forces and their slumbers sings:

> For every thing that lives is holy, life delights in life;
> Because the soul of sweet delight can never be defiled . . .

The tones of speech offer the first reawakenings of primordial dissuasions and release from ancient and constantly imperiling propaganda as well as poised endurances by which to disarm the forces and ruling slumbers which Blake understood would enslave us in our time. Their energy informs us that once we are able to realize and proclaim that the Behemoth Rich who have stolen our Time and World and the Deepest Hells of violence they are willing to unleash to preserve themselves no longer matter to our lives that we can in that instance begin to imagine another world and to cut ourselves away from the Mystery tyrants and their waves of foaming blood until "not one" as the poet says in his "Four Zoas" is "left on Earth." We have "Jerusalem" "The Four Zoas" the horror strangeness of "The Book of Ahania" so often accompanied by very thin readings to this day. But Blake (as Shakespeare and Dante) seems to read his Age as few rarely have. His "Epics" and "Prophecies" in the magnitude of their challenge presents a new storehouse of perils measured defined weighed as taxonomic specimens along with their paleontology no matter how complex or murky. The recital is often devastating in terms of a possible mutagenic apocalypse of Being and the angelic confrontation Blake knew must be made Public in order to invent himself in the force of his own recognitions to make Life come true once more. He identifies a crisis of immemorial Beginnings and their endurance and makes of it a new composure to be shared and used.

There seems in this too, a further stance of consideration in relationship to Paleolithic art. When one regards the practices of various American tribal Peoples and their studies can this open up a new range of cooperative resonances toward much of the now ever enlarging orphaned storehouse of human experience? I am thinking for instance of how an individual tribal woman or man would have studied as I understand the information a pond or small lake and the lore such a body of water invoked from one generation to another over hundreds and even thousands of years. Each sharing population would have observed the other creatures; animals, plants, insects, fish, birds, and passage of those generations noting the cycles of health and disease, new migrants and transformations, the forms of weather, colors of sky. The documentation afforded a sense of projective imagination and by that applicable and even masterful meanings. As example one might think of a young girl who learns of such a pond or lake from her mother and grandmother and because of that extends their calling to fascination life-long care and womanly lore. She notes over her lifetime the whole creaturely web including herself and expanding that active intellectual/visionary achievement imagines more particularly what this immediate geography might look like in a thousand or five thousand years-and what would be alive extending the energy of that care far beyond anything our own assumptions can presently hold or dismiss. Such senses of future personally felt and extended, the rigor of a Self foreseeing the continued living fullness of a world was part of communal sounding and creative extremity inseparable from daily life. Do the Cro-Magnon images carry a similar sense of creative extremities and generative call for awareness in order to avoid the tyrannies of barrenness that otherwise wait for human generations who might attempt to enslave and conscript what was so long ago recorded in those caves into cravings for sustained ruins and is this another way we can regard this art as it confronts the constantly transforming human aptitudes for oppression?

Olson's "March 6th, 1968" poem about "an actual earth of value" holds some of these repositories of courage:

an actual earth of value to

construct one, from rhythm to

image, and image is knowing, and

knowing, Confucius says, brings one

to the goal: nothing is possible without

doing it.   It is where the test lies, malgre

all the thought and all the pell-mell of

proposing it. Or thinking it out or living it

ahead of time

In that too, what vivid life application might lessen the real conspiracy in which we live, the one Lawrence identifies in his strange "St. Mawr":

> ... to live in absolute physical safety, whilst willing the minor disintegration of all positive living ...

gradually but inexorably releasing ourselves from life engendering scruples. And in these passages Lawrence does ask questions which do have a numen about them which shake or help to shake the founding contaminations converting the word "HUMANITY" into an unbearable and despised homelessness neither dictionary nor memory can allow in lowliness of scorns we heap upon it:

> But now where is the flame of dangerous, forward-pressing nobility in men?

"Dead, dead" the novelist poet and painter answers and nothing now to illuminate the way but the "feeble light of exhaustion" given off by "laissez-faire."
Are the Caves an image of dangerous forward pressing nobility?
Or *malgre* as Fanny Howe might have it containing the further burdens of Olson's word and embodying her own Non-Male depths of a yearning

"one third" refusing to exploit the luring Decompositions and their lordly
steely commands:

> Come, tinkers, among droves of acorn trees
>
> Be only one third needful, O
>
> Name the things whereby we hope
>
> Before the story scatters. A cardinal
>
> Is red for fever where you passed
>
> The suffering world's faith
>
> Is a scandal. Tests of facts
>
> Bring dread to aptitude
>
> You who loved the people and the world
>
> Tell us our failings and if we're home

Wednesday October 5th 2005: My B-day 61. Clay called and Gail gave me
a new sweater and shirt. Delicious!

Sunday October 9th 2005: Friday we went to Pacific Beach, spent a quiet
afternoon at the shore listening to the Ocean, watching Sky and motion of
Sun breathing the planetary Winds. Saturday we purchased a "ready-
made" storage building for tools, supplies, other necessities.

The Bush doctrines are in a state of chaos. The central argument and presumption that establishing "democracy" will stifle the Iraq insurgency and establish stability can be directly traced to this man's words, "Bring it on." A fool smothered in his Christian cult delivered the dare and the dare has been met in the incarnations of Zigguratic Murder and Lion Violences to scour the conqueror at the core of his living energies and strengths.

There is a cuneiform tablet from the Old Babylonian period, ca. 1740 B.C. currently housed at the University of Pennsylvania Museum of Archaeology. It is a "Lamentation over the Destruction of Sumer and Ur." The agonizing presence of the Unspeakable recorded in this ancient fascinating mud work speaks directly to the apparitional convulsions rupturing out in our 3445 years separation from the sack of these cities:

> Ningirsu wasted Sumer like milk poured
> to the dogs
> Revolt descended upon the land, some-
> thing that no one had ever known,
> Something unseen, which has no name,
> something that could not be fathomed.
> The god of that city turned away, its shep-
> herd vanished.
> The people, in fear, could barely breath,
> The storm immobilizes them; the storm
> does not let them return; the time of
> captivity does not pass.

" ... like milk poured/to the dogs ..." seems still fresh and first knowledge stranded as it is in this ceramic archive whispering to us with a hovering lucidity over freakish slaughter; no immunity offered down through the millennia, non given in any world marked by ruthless waste. And whoever the survivor is who speaks here, Her or His witness of the always sinister leftovers has the cold-eyed tone of precisions which must accompany the nightmare fires of cities transformed into burning meat without any interfering ornamentation, a compressed epic concerned with telling a story no matter its revulsions and as Zukofsky might have said the writer keeping eyes and ears "fastened" (his wonderful verb) to what is immediately seen and felt and to let that and that only command the intelligence otherwise what human and humane sound can possibly traverse such scale of time and disintegrations.

I also in this consideration remember Gordon Matta Clark's sculptures from the early 1970s when that unusual artist took a chain saw and began cutting apart houses creating spaces shadows lines arousals that lent a new mystery to the common "home"; restored what we think of domesticity to a haunted ground and even cemetery-like flickering giving to these "America Spaces" as deep a murmuring as the Grand Canyon or the Great Plains.

Me and Gail listened to an analysis by a female journalist from CBS (can't for shit sakes remember her name) whose sense was really penetrant of the Bush administration's control of information and any possible feeling. Iraq because of that is so distant a thing that no one cares about the war. Does such plunge into empty blankness mean we will never be allowed to know how disfigured we are and will be condemned to be and is it necessary for our health to know about the disfigurement and to reckon it as a central fact of our lives?

Bush also threatened to veto the McCain Bill banning all forms of interrogation behavior lying outside the parameters of the Geneva Convention guidelines. McCain's reason for the legislation – that the Nation's image has suffered grievous harm – not actual flesh and blood persons quivering in the vast dread of our punishment maintenance systems. Blake would have called this division, this descent from the Feeling Brain a "Hermaphroditic Condensation" that can only take place when reality is:

" . . . cut asunder by Jealousy & Pity . . ."

Tuesday October 11th 2005: Walked Lake Murray this morning. The sky divided by an intense wash of blue and a high bank of cooling fog. The cormorants have also returned, as well as a large contingent of mallards. The cormorants swimming in a rhythmic unison dove and then re-appeared, their snake-like heads tense and nervous, their diving formations and emergencies were almost spell-like in a mathematical sequence of appearance/disappearance then appearance again transforming the surface of the lake into a play of immediate mysterious shadow, the bird-life erect, honed, and intricately sharp in its communal hunting disciplines.

An impressive small article today on a group of lawyers called "The Prison Law Office" in San Quentin California. These are the people responsible for the recent landmark decisions against the California adult and juvenile prison systems and the ghoulish abuses which have assumed a force of normality in these allowably consecrated hells.

A sickening photograph of New Orleans policemen beating an adult African American male. The police violence was video taped and the man, repeatedly punched, is named Robert Davis, a retired elementary school teacher.

Friday October 14th 2005: The temperature reached 104 degrees. Air clear. Pine Cone dry. Drains the skin. Everything stunned by the Santa Anas.

Wasn't anything in the coastal deserts mountains jungles those women wouldn't examine. From every inch of textile they went seemingly to every inch of land. What they were after was fiber and the qualities of the yield. Wasn't a wild or domestic animal, wild or domestic plant they didn't render over into a personal study in the way they became mathematicians and chemists botanists and engineers. The forms of weaving they bore translated from their looms outward into knot coded symbols, identities, numbers surged to the shores of writing and legendary suspension bridges. With the amounts of thread spun over those thousands of years you could go sail the hydrogen seas of Jupiter, uncurl the same spindle in the hundred thousand year cannibal storm spewing over the dwarf faces of the cyanide seas of this Earth with their geysers of earliest mysteries about the beginning of beginnings lying in some deep freeze birth debris remote demons bit each others' eyes for.

Sunday October 16th 2005: 11:20am 62 degrees. A dramatic transformation of weather. Friday the gauge registered 104 and today it is sprinkling; a cool wind pushed through our wind chimes. News of terrible flooding in the Northeast and unprecedented hurricanes in the Southern hemisphere of the Americas. Bush forever ready with photo-ops.
"And men are less than the green-fly sucking the stems of the bush, so long as they live by business and bread alone. Parasites on the face of the earth . . ." Reading about the prisons: "Between 1982 and 2001, arrests in the United States increased by 13%, yet the number of inmates in federal and state prisons surged 228%. The total number of Americans in prison, jail, on probation or on parole soared from 400,000 in 1970 to 1.8 million in 1980 and to 6.7 million in 2002. About 13 million Americans have served time for a felony conviction."

Monday October 17th 2005: 10:00am 68 degrees. Overcast with patches of blue sky. The turn of temperatures has also been accompanied by the emergence of a coastal desert light, subtle, at once wet-dry, lending a difference to each sunrise and sunset.

Bush is dragging his feet over Katrina somehow hoping the "market" will right the ship. A dishonor to the Soul to hear this man's voice see this man's face.

Now 11:50am. Black skies, ravens searching for shelter rain coming in big wind-swept drops.

Thursday October 20th 2005: Overcast 62 degrees. Watched a "Frontline" special Tuesday night on Abu Ghraib. The whole thing an unspeakable lurking poisoned sea drowning the well-being of both nations drowning the well-being of the World.

A string of pieces on the California prisons in the LA Times. The head reads: "More than 10 years after the law was enacted, the latest study finds no direct link between harsher sentencing and crime reduction . . ." One quarter of the state's prisoners (40,000 women and men) are doing time for a second or third strike. "Most are in prison for non-serious or non-violent crimes. The original measure ("Three Strikes") also raised the punishment requirements for "second strikers" requiring that the usual sentence be doubled and that at least 80% of the time be served before parole may be considered. The law remains popular with politicians and the public . . ." "Popularity" can be identified in this instance as one of the "monsters of the deeps" presently possessing and making a "Fiend" of our communal selves.

Friday October 21st 2005: Foggy cool morning. Walked around Lake Murray and to our delight three white pelicans have returned. Beautiful creatures with black feathers on the undersides of their wings. And a magnificent osprey perched on a tree top with its wings unfolded and hanging downward to dry; an incredible pose almost totemic in its raw stillness and power.

A.M. Josephy Jr., the journalist and chronicler of the American Indians has died at the age of 91. His fascinations began with an anger over the fact that the Lewis and Clarke story had never been told through the perceptions of the Indians themselves.

There is a discouraging headline today; a bill in Congress which shields gun manufacturers and gun sellers from lawsuits. The immunity for this industry allows the People to take a further step into the Web of Death that has been woven with such care and patience for us all:

> ... this
> desperate
> ugly
> cruel
> land this Nation
> which never
> lets anyone
> come to
> shore ...

and

> ... how many waves
> of hell and death and
> dirt and shit
> meaningless waves of hurt and punished lives shall America
> be nothing but the story of
>   not al all her successes –
>   I have been – Leroy has been
> as we genetic failure are
> successes, here

it isn't interesting,
Yankees – European, Chinese

What is at heart, turning
beating itself out leftward
in hell to know heaven
in the filthy land
in this foul country where
    human lives are so much trash
    it is the dirty restlessness
    of fear and shame . . .

And an end to Hell
    and even to Heaven

                   Charles Olson February 7th 1966

. . . None of us
sustaining being . . .
          slips
into the specialization of
    Darkness . . .

Does this small second passage of Olson's tell of the more subtle crushing world divisions taking place with even greater exaggeration than what previous generations may have experienced; what before could have been defined as conscience vs. the covert secretly venomous invasions of daily life that ravish and drain each woman and man in advanced predatory industrial cultures slowly but which in this time have each become the vindictive disfigurements of species poised on their opposite summits each of them equally and helplessly perverse in the carefully crafted malevolences which everyone of us, no matter where we want to or might turn away from the strangulations, gratify? And though one can say that Olson's 19th century graph of wrongs, compelling as they are, are not enough. Here that measure does extend into the present frictions and upheavals of the untellable alien removes glistening with their conceited madness and Olson's call for immediate present awareness is not a withered stem but fresh companionable fire.

Monday October 24th 2005: A group of US soldiers has burned bodies of so-called Taliban insurgents in Afghanistan. There is a seamless passage of ghoul violences from the preppy rulers with their Harvard Princeton Yale U of Chicago degrees to these lowest sadly brain damaged grunts. Both spectrums of Ulro Delusions as Blake said in his "Milton Book the First":

> They dance around the dying, & they drink the howl & groan
> They catch the shrieks in cups of gold, they hand them to one another

Blake's transformation of the "shrieks" into a drunken delectation evokes the groveling exultant Death Clusterings. Gail and I talking of these facts along with the sense that the specie's central nervous system may be an evolutionary dead end – Gail said the terrible crisis of the civilization has become "a consumption procurement system" applicable only to itself as sensory response.

One of the most important stories of the last three years. A minute notice in the wire service reports in the back pages of the LA Times. The number of women sent to prisons in America has risen dramatically in the last two years. Women now make up 7% of all inmates on both the federal and state levels. Since 2004 the numbers are up 4% compared with 2003, or more than double the 1.8% increase for men (as of today May 24th 2006 the prison population in America has increased to 2.2 million people meaning that in the years 2004-2005 which this writing examines 1,085 inmates were added each week to the prison population. And though men were 10 to 11 times more likely than women to be thrown away, the numbers of women are growing at a faster rate. The racial make-up of the Industry remains for the most part unchanged. In the 25 to 29 age grouping, 11.9% of Black males are in prison. For Hispanics males the number is 3.9%, for White males, 1.7%. Though prison inmates are barred from voting in 48 states state legislatures habitually count inmates as "residents" to pad legislative districts where the local population is too small and through this increases the power of rural districts where the prisons are built. The gerrymandering has helped the Republican Party, for instance, in northern New York State maintain its majority in the State Senate and to exercise a disproportionate influence in the affairs of that state. The Republican leadership of New York has argued that counting inmates as residents of these isolated districts is no different than counting college students as temporary residents of dormitories. In other words the unbearable lowliness of the spread wave and its unrelenting erasure has reached a form of perfected deceit; the democracy mutating from prison outwards as Toroid and Toroidal Circulation).

A possible larger question – are numbers such as these indicative of what can and will be done at Guantanamo Abu Ghraib and larger Black Sites such as Iraq Afghanistan Iran and any other geography of choice that will be designated as either a Person or Nation of Interest to use Ashcroft's tone given the "salamandrine" immensities of language stranded in a nowhere " ... and like the black pebble on the enraged beach ..." of Blake's vision. Can what we now are beginning to do to our own populations of women be done to the populations of the Nations in Waiting for these and other variations of "Shock and Awe"?

Are such numbers now a prophetic tool, pythonic memorabilia extending from the creature processions of the Wondrous/Sullen Caves?

Tuesday October 25th 2005: Sun struggling to appear. Rosa Parks has died peacefully in her home near Detroit. She was 92 and no personal refusal in the history of the country has done more to change the country's murderous racisms or to impose at least some partial recognition which sadly remains only partial as witness on this same day the case of Stanley "Tookie" Williams whose plea for clemency is ignored. Again, here is a single figure, who, like no other, can speak out against the gang world which has swallowed the lives of countless young women and men and their families, their communities. The white world wants his corpse as proper business transaction to recall Edward Dorn's truthful upturnings of the unbearable savagery enrooted in the depths of the color codes which have no beginning and no end and the forms of worship we constantly invent for them. Modular steel no matter the shape; chains, shackles, astrophysics for the highest available sensitivity as perfection technology once twice whatever it takes take a close look take a closer look at our worldwide offender management systems pick and choose the applications of mix-and-match philosophy mix-and-match convivialities of the viciousness and dread so superbly arrived sentencing everything before it and after it to obsolescence.

Today the 2000th Soldier has fallen in Iraq and thousands of the Wounded have fearful injuries which will require a lifetime of intensive care.

Thursday October 27th 2005: 10:05pm. Coming home from work we saw two beautiful coyotes walking sniffing snooping mapping our neighborhood with a kind of contemptuous leisure. Such a relief to know we've got this company and recalling the sad question Creeley asked near the end of his life about us, what will the world be like when it is only ourselves having done away with the other Sisters and Brothers of the Creation and left to stammer in our loss?

And what about physical endurance? Those born to it let the body learn of itself to weather loneliness, the vocations of the sun carving its ends and penalties bringing forth a waterless stillness. My mother hated it. The heat starting at her ankles in the mornings and rising slowly until she'd head off every few years leaving behind her dried yucca Christmas trees, saying she'd grown bored with pine, wanted this placement of the desert right next to the hearth itself, an unapproachable skeleton preempting any of her dreams of moisture guttering the phantasies of an American Christmas replacing it with the recklessly leafless, fleshless.

A woman's workbasket from 700AD. My mother examined it and realized she'd created a basket almost the twin of this older women's thing. And the similarities didn't stop there. Both were filled with needles, spools of dyed thread ready for a woman's fingers, experiments, teeth, and toes. She dreamed about those needles. Knitted shawls, dresses, pulled shapes from the air around her hands as if what they were, were the deepest snows embedded in her skin, the earlier wrists like her own, delicate, brown, suppled for these inventions. She studied what those women did. Considered them ancestresses even though they were Andean, not the Aztec of her emergences, but blood nonetheless swelling in wonders, then to be trickled into parched floods of heat narrowing to troughs between mountains or planets where no rumor of sympathy forages. Those ladies from Huaca Prieta to Cuzco fashioned skills over five thousand years that seemed for my mother to have no placement anywhere other than the Maule and the San Lorenzo. Color, design, intricacy here are spun and woven so finely that the number of threads reached as much as five thousand for every inch of that hand and eye held labor. Some have gone to far as to say that the foundations of this world start with weaving and the *mamakuna* and only after will eating appear with its alter necessities.

But my mother also went to search out a single thread, one unlike any other on the planet at the time of its conception. She told herself she was going to be the eyes of her husband, but really it was to see what she believed was a project mathematically designed by women who came upon hydrologic formula no civilization even began to think about until the appearances of the twentieth century. She didn't know which came first but felt the dreams in number and formula began with shifting earth and catastrophic rains. No one can affix any precise detail to those years from nine to twelve hundred A.D. when the Moche River went from being a thing drunk by land which got no more than a half inch rain fall a year to a thing which gulped any geology in front of it two miles and more wide, fifty foot deep in a trajectory to the Peru Trench. She saw those Chimu women examining the results, spinning their minds in order to alter landscapes as answer to the Moche's hunger in proportion, theory, sustenance, and that they were capable of sending an emissary, not exactly of this world, to get the valleys under other earthly rule they needed. The local rival king was ripe not just for seduction but disintegration. The mistqueen they conjured really wanted him and as his own gods watched what she had him do to her there, passed the binoculars until the lenses were fogged over with what makes creatures into the beautiful disappointments they seem never not to be. His gods up and delivered a thirty day rain for the dreams of their king and food of his people and as the women knew, knowing what men do, the resort to disfigurement in king or god-mind would outlast every other exhilaration.

Land and irrigation was what it was for. To stop the periodic gluttony of the rivers and coastal lifting with its far sharper and more subtle appetites causing wells and rivers to become mysteriously unreachable, become the spit of stingrays. The Indians of those cities dove into the antarctic currents that brought up sea-lion, penguin, and surfer's ear. She figured that'd be about right having spent some of her years worrying that one day she'd have to hear a story of the sea she'd never be able to escape about sons or nephews caught in a run of fifteen footers and taken by the sirens there who like grabbing mortals by their rib cages as if they were nightflowers or fireflies closing up for the first bursts of dawn.

Accompanying hearing impairment when sea diving was first accomplished from too much immersion in the ice-watered seas were the initial decorative textiles in all the Americas, the initial experiments of their kind in shades of browns, tans, and whites. It was a use of everything they were after from the purest sea-bird shit off their coastal islands to the most elegant vampire bat hair mixed with parrots' tails aching for arrival through their wrists and fingers and tinnitus of their deep dives.

As to that thread my mother came to see, it was about female excesses so huge that the dust after nine hundred years hadn't settled and as far as she was concerned nine hundred more couldn't be enough. From early on she knew what it meant to be hooked up to roses having as she had to to watch her husband search for rain or sprinkles, cloudburst or whatever might be tied to the isotopic ratios of oxygen and hydrogen. His stare at the sun-up runs of cloudless sky almost caused a boil of jealousy while he'd murmur in the after-seconds of their simplest intimacies not caring whether he was actually out of range, an equation about what any day was "No water / No life" the two compound adjectives and their nouns headed to luckless drift where the final vowel wavers as some hobbled crumb.

She told the farmer when she saw the fifty mile long canal, the bewildered statement about a day he seemed to carry in the driest canyons of his brain, welled up as his voice in hers, as if it were the bellowing of a storm snuck out to strike it rich or go goddamned bust in an uglier destiny which seemed just completely unable to find any shelter. The farmer liked her language when she was like that, staring off, he thought, from some present curvature toward the volcanoes where her people came from, made her half dry and sexy with the breakages of her past he knew she'd never recover, stare into what she thought was the communal genius of women till she and her tongue and what came to lick him also into a half life turned to stone.

If any water supply could ever be said to be steady then here on our California alluvial fans it meant steadily dying, diving farther in moisturelessness and his nights as a young farmer, tacking up signs in our town about soil and water conservation, meetings over agriculture rich lands gone jet hot to mortgage-a-minute brokery, and wherever he could balance any of the estranging accompaniment of real-estate that ate valleys, mountains, rivers; made a caterpillar devoured forest seem like the frailest agitation or remnant silhouette, fleshless death corpse of the land to be merely sniffed against the equation in my mother's eyes over drawer-fulls of delicately leathered gloves and spewing shit boats every spring come to the fields around her fine house with their storms of clotted manure.

She knew about the race of giants in the highlands and the absence of women among them. Apparently their longings attained to equally tall and thorny starvations and grown close to their hungers they went a little exotic, going out from the mountain fastness as drag queens in search of lovers and it didn't matter if the lowland strangers were giants or not just as long as they were boys, short, tall, or fat. Such things often became a tradition. Days get reserved. Sacred ones for pleasure where men in the present fondle the offspring of those giants and if the ecstasy was good enough why then you could go up for that evening with the Cloud Beings of the Milky Way who'd take you to the farthest sex realms this section of the creation had to offer.

Here against the Andean foothills some crucial omission had occurred. The sanctions for rape and exclusion had not fallen yet so completely over women and what their minds held. My mother believed the intricacies of their weaving and chemistry brought them to the edges of an advanced physics allowing for the creation of a gorgeous failure unadorned by anything but its own emptiness as testimony, a woman-mind loathsome now and unbelievable to our world but before the terrible deadnesses set in they were able to lure precisions, wreathe and mate them to the fevers of another wakefulness and its human poise drowned in this time:

Rabid saliva at work
Remote paraphernalia of wrath
In whose name
For what is under sky?

She scribbled this question after her name on a fancy Lima Hotel guest list. The references we knew were to one of her horse master early nineteenth century Californios aunts who collected as it was told to us in our mid-twentieth century childhoods various kinds of reptiles which included rattle and coral snakes, black widows and tarantulas, deadly scorpions but came up against old Atropos herself in the form of a gila monster that bit her and from which symptoms she suffered and died it is further said drowning in her own saliva the venom as it did producing a small personal but effective ocean one of the first recordings of this Fate, Clothos and Lachesis as dumb struck by the weirdness as everyone else visible or invisible having to do with this business on Earth. And though my father had respected her separateness, she knew in this time it could be nothing more than a private encroachment on his behalf she had allowed, the most depleting patronage as if the whole secret between themselves was a tarantula hawk searching for lairs of its hairy spiders, some fuckin Noah out there flying in the driest hills with a bad sting and a weird fetus sucking the huge spiders from the inside out and taking their secret time.

The frontal walls of the Andes start their immense thrust near the point where ocean touches land. For the Chimu women, the wanton inevitableness of the results and its leftovers describes only the short-breathed tolerances of the dying come to know this heave in the body, foraging for air, and finding so little. What control of arable sediment it might've encompassed in this glare of expert soil managements carrying its female whispers back at least seven or eight thousand years is only a speculation in the desert severities of another planet earth where every clod of dirt and what it was worth according to a whole set of replenishments that looks like a petrified nest robbery now, came under the exact tendings of hands and feet and a long range experimental intelligence. As a California rancher and farmer's son I seem often to return to the thought of farming or urban gardening and the long term senses of what the word agriculture might be in relation to its previous definitions and usages; the art of cultivating the soil knowing that soil itself in all its thousands of varieties is the seat of life and full of mystery as its Sister Ocean. As a boy I spent much time in the San Joaquin Valley and as a man I still find great joy in driving those California Plains observing the crops and the distantly looming Sierras. But the Valley and its agriculture as I knew it has been custom re-profiled. "Farming" in this, one of the richest soil banks on the planet, is seen as a mass sterilization project that has envenomated the air and ground water. The cause: pesticides herbicides and fumigants. There are over 700 pesticides presently in use and most of these chemical agents contain volatile organic compounds or VOCs which in the process of evaporation become key components of ozone and other hazardous air-borne pollutants as huge tractors plow night and day at 50 miles per hour. Perhaps some of the most poisonous of the "agents" are the fumigants; highly poisoous gases that account for at least a quarter of all pesticides applied on California crops. The major fumigants are methyl bromide, metam sodium, and chloropicrin. These agents can cause both neurological and reproductive damage. They are first injected as gases before crops are planted in order to sterilize the soil.

Methyl bromide describes what is called a "Broad Spectrum" pesticide used to control insects, weeds, rodents, pathogens. It is a colorless odorless gas and can be applied under pressure directly to the soil as a liquid. As a "Broad Spectrum" agent it is divided into three families:

"Sanitizer": Significantly reducing bacterial populations in the inanimate environment but does not eliminate all microorganisms.
"Disinfectant": Destroys or eliminates a specific species of microorganisms but not necessarily spores in the inanimate environment.
"Sterilant": A substance that eliminates all forms of microbial life in the inanimate environment.
Metam Sodium is applied to five major commercial crops:
Carrots
Tomatoes
Potatoes
Bell Peppers
Onions

When one thinks of the term "Immigration" and the human beings who are manipulated by both the ruling economic forces in Mexico and the United States then those women and men and children who will do the work "Americans" will no longer do are the direct receivers of the symptoms specifically related to the application of these "agents." While a teenager growing up in Arizona my father shifted his farming expertise from the hybridization of roses to the wider and more profitable crops of lettuce potatoes and cotton. The "Bracero Program" was then at maximum implementation importing "workers" from Mexico at low wage and supplying housing quarters often so crude that those spaces were only one more health hazard encompassing both the sleeping and waking worlds. There were as a matter of course barrels of "chemical agents" stored in on-site supply barns always at the ready for any emergency that might threaten to reduce profits. The warning signs on those containers were written in English with no thought that the "immigrants" assigned to handle such dangers would be completely unable to decipher the threat. One of those sadly nameless men told to prepare a spray rig unscrewed the protective seal of a barrel without a gas mask and died in his own vomit a few minutes later. It is a story and image that has haunted me and my senses of "farming," and whatever that word once meant seems no matter what I might otherwise wish, to circle around the betrayal of this humble and very foreign man whose suffering was recorded as merely contempt by other farmers who thought the "Bracero" stupid and hardly worth their smirk. The mixtures of racism and chemistry emanating from the lung blistering clouds of World War I did their job superbly that day. I wrote out of this in one of my first fully realized poems:

Crazy farmers Crazy Farmers
squirting brain death
everytime the sun threatened to piss butterflies.

The direct symptoms of metam sodium poisoning are:

Headache dizziness
Irritation of the eyes nose throat
Nausea diarrhea
Shortness of breath, chest tightness

More importantly this chemical is identified as a "Bad Actor" meaning that it is as described in the various literatures "highly acutely toxic." The adverbs in this phrase are stranded in a floatation around the membranous adjective as unreckoned emission. It is at once a carcinogen, a ground water pollutant and a "reproductive – developmental toxicant" where now the adjectives in this second descriptive phrase before their noun seem like slightly powdered thin-skinned shaky hands barely able to hold even the nearest air. I have no idea what exact "agent" killed that long-ago "Bracero" who worked for my father. But I do know that he may as well have unscrewed the war-head of a poisoned gas artillery shell mixed with agribusiness, the two theatres having so long ago combined into twins whose aerosol dynamics defaces any mythological attempt to recompose their realms of disturbance and loss into recognizable appearance for we who are living it as cost for prosperity or the "we" who will bear the after-world of its having been.

Chloropicrin is a "slightly oily colorless or faintly yellow liquid." These parts of speech are so slippery that whatever is being described here at this point of vital necessity for us who are the Breathers and Inhalers and Drinkers as an act of language is left prostrate and withered. Chloropicrin is highly poisonous if inhaled. It was used first for military purposes in World War I as a chemical weapon known as "PS' by the British "KLOP" by the Germans and "Aquinite" by the French who have made their name for this "agent" sound almost jewel-like in its death precisions. It is a pow-erful and deadly pulmonary agent and in its soil application can cause "blueish skin" dermatitis corneal ulcerations and abrasions pediatric reactive airway diseases ultraviolet sensitivity and blindness. Are we any longer "farming" or are we waging a mass sterilization policy against the "inanimate environment" without any definition of what such an "envi-ronment" might accurately be and what corporations or groups of corpo-rately sponsored "growers" as we now might call "Farming" a "Management Development Enthusiasm" have decided upon such identities and can "Real Estate Development" and it mythologies within the borders of this consideration be seen as part of the family of "Broad Spectrum" Agents?

My mother before the propaganda the chemical industry sent my father, a Jew himself, about the sterilization of the "inanimate" considered the articulation and reach of the previous women a shift in mind sistered to the shifts of mountains. That extremity she thought cut as deep into them as the rivers drying up before their eyes. So those women as my mother wrote in her diary touched the jurisdictions of sand dune and sun-cracked foothills personally to come up with a fifty mile stretch of winding tortured canal to take water from the River Chicama to the River Moche through a scab of uplift no engineered design had ever undertaken. The terms of description for what those women attempted goes blunt. Where the "La Cumbre" runs it looks like the sun bit every part of that landscape, got so hungry one day for some better to forget reason and caused a permanent local evaporation no truce comes to still. If one ever does it'll probably be maimed, penciled with a warning about galactic explosions and their invisible remnant lusts come to claw the valleys of this or other planets, cast a signature, then peak off into other distributions a billion years away.

Weaving the "Canal" into this place meant an unobscured communion with mathematics, precision engineering, human labor, and social cost. Aquaduct and embankment were constructed with a never before known residence in cobble, fire broken boulder, hard packed dirt fill. Some of those supportive banks as they weave through sixty degree sloped mountains are at least ten stories in height, each section gouged with numerical formula and nerve, every stone of it a hardly visited waste even today. But as my mother walked it she realized they never got to play the design. Not a single gallon creased most of those miles of grade and hydrologic reformation. There are echoes of flow tests, on-going irrigation experiments, simulation runs. Why the shut down? No one can say. But my mother thought there was nothing those Chimu women had not foreseen. They could alter flow rate, change the profile of curves to avoid embankment collapse, downshift water speed with hydraulic jumps of perfectly placed boulders. What methods did they employ to calculate the heights of level for intake and outlet over this span? No one knows this either about the mystery of separation between the two points those women worked on. They used up more than two unrelenting centuries and eight generations of themselves and others for this one single thread. For my mother it was like Etowa with those two figurines as mathematically shattered halves looking out over

Yucca Flats watching the numbers and their variations that had been thought to hold one fate be brought to the gluttony of another eating its way backwards and suspending all of what was meant to have been light. The seated staring couple dug out of their mound braced in their re-arrival to string the equations through their teeth in order to take a clearer measure of the twentieth century American world which had spawned them.

She came back from one of those visits, played solitaire, dressed, put on a pair of her leather gloves every morning, took a black coral cigarette holder to the game every morning. Her living room became a one-player high stakes unlimited casino. My father picked me and my sister up for those after weeks, cooked us dinner, let us ride on an old white mule he kept around until the game was run through.

Sunday October 30th 2005: Last night 10:00pm went out to see Mars on the Eastern horizon close and cold. Below it peculiar trembling Pleiades and just upthrusted on the same plane great Orion. Wonders of Winter's approach!

Information this morning about the army's disposal of lethal weapons on the coasts of the Nation. The piece begins with the narrative of an incident involving bomb disposal technicians from Dover Air Base in Delaware who were deployed to dismantle an artillery shell filled with mustard gas in a "solid" form; three of those "technicians were "injured." No details apart from the distant vaguery except that what was long ago feared by the few military experts in the know has come to pass – chemical weapons that the army dumped at sea decades ago have finally ended up on shore. These secret dumping programs are far more extensive than previously known.

> 64 million pounds of active nerve gas and mustard gas have been dumped at sea along with 400,000 active chemical bombs and 500,000 tons of radio
> active waste,

These chemical agents will pose a hazard for generations.

The army doesn't any longer know where all the sites might be because it
has lost or misplaced vital records.

This "secret" weapons dumping program spanned the decades from 1944
(the year of my birth) to 1970. The weapons were and are:

Hazardous to transport

Expensive to store

Too dangerous to bury

Difficult to destroy

The questions raised by this multiple choice array can barely find proper
or coherent utterance. The complete betrayal and disregard of a Nation's
health, the haphazard, malignant laxity posing as refined management, the
loutish belittlements practiced by each generation of generals and politicians lurching toward the continent's seashores. Where to call but to an
archaic vocabulary, Middle English or passages that may involve ourselves,
the "Books of Chilam Balam" addressing the cycles of fate in the Americas
and its references to the:

> smooth
>
> Punisher ("Cex Ah num")
>
> Collected by the "Winds of the earth."

Can such vocabulary belong as one reads of the "Ah taxtal" "The Flat-
teners" or the "Ah actal" "The Diminisher" who cast the word of the red
and White nightmare into Time?

Screeching sorcerers of prosperities vomit splitting the throat   sold by
the sons

>   to the sons   selling the born   as of a we are torn chickens
>   Piled   the   Stinking   Period

>   Our trust   transformed into the   New

Calendars of   Poisoned   Centuries

Suffer   Girls   Suffer   Boys
Slavery to have been born into the ancient American Word "TOON"
Whose meaning is both "Secret" and "Testicle" Rulers with Poisoned
Balls aligned to   OKAM BAL CAH   "Gone Is The World"
Mourning   Bowls   at   the   entrances   to   our   Cities
Covered with Centipedes

Monday October 31st 2005: It is 12:45pm temperature hovering at 97
degrees, hard winds blowing from the south. Last night Mars, the Pleiades,
Orion and, I think, Saturn sailing the night sky and hot, boiling Venus on
the sunset horizon, a hovering, throbbing trance-dense flame exuding what
orders of ancient fire someone on the planet may still know?

Monday November 7th 2005: 9:49am, 71 degrees. Last week Gail had a
chance to meet the great ceramicist, Richard Shaw. To talk, watch him
work, observe, become friends.
Friday and Saturday we met with friends, went first to Yuma for the night,
and then early the following morning drove back across the Border and
into the Pacheco Reserve, one of the starkest most mysterious wildernesses
we've ever seen. Area: the Chocolate Mountains. The Park is rarely visited.
We were part of small group and our guide was a geologist from San Diego
State University who took us on a great journey of explanations and
wonders from the early Jurassic to the middle Pleistocene. We walked over
Cretaceous and Miocene lava flows, Oligocene and Cretaceous sand dunes,
Miocene alluvial sands and cores of disappeared mountains. We examined
Cretaceous pyroclastic lava gone white as Grandma's hair, and ancient, no
longer active faults scarring the sides of canyon walls. We could see the
striated, giant fossilized rubbings of planetary segments a hundred million
years old which left us speechlessly amazed. The environment of this space

is as it has been for at least 50,000 to 60,000 years when a great climatic change occurred and the elephants, lions, sabre-toothed tigers, camel, short-faced bears, dire wolves and other fauna and flora migrated north to the L.A. Basin. Ground sloth may have stayed on for another 20,000 years, but the summer heat was dangerously prohibitive except near the swamps and riverine tides of the Colorado, a Miocene river approximately 10 million years old. Think back to whatever that Dawn might be and you could guess, though it had business sure as shit, even Death was a little younger then as it watched this wild thread of Water cut and slice and flirt with the Appearances.

And though the temperatures of our early winter visit seemed unnoticeably easy you had to take account, couldn't forget where you were; we had to drink water constantly, the subtle but unrelenting moistureless winds made you feel your own witherings and made you feel you'd better hear those witherings. Wasn't ugly, but check the radiator just the same, make sure no ancient teratornis rides the thermals of an Oligocene cliff. Disorientation lurks in the simplest shadows where the lone experienced or inexperienced wanderer can hitch that ride the Chocolate Mountain tortoises offer. We went through desert valleys filled with large lakes, swamps, and grass shrouded shores fed by the meanders of the Colorado. Lone egrets mallards a golden eagle or two swooping but no migratory flocks and the invading silence at once delicate and brutal simmering in its clarity and offering no shelter. There are lions, wild burros, big horn sheep, bobcats, tortoise, rattlesnakes and secrets never to be unlocked. One could spend ten lifetimes and not even begin to comprehend the great story. As I recall instances of that journey, one moment arises, one where we found a flowering desert Acacia covered with bees, the perfumes of that tree carrying a sweet quickened charge of enriched newness and lures hovering just beyond the late afternoon shadows of a huge Oligocene alluvial formation now transformed into dramatically layered cliffs. A large covey of quail suddenly appeared out of those bordering shadows with their headdresses. We lived in an isolate valley in the Catskill Mountains for many years and saw intimately much of that eastern forest wildlife. On our hikes we often came across wild turkey or chipmunks or deer or the very rare Bluebird that had literally never seen a human being. Some stared in astonishment as if the ugly something we were had caused a temporary paralysis and such tender vulnerability made us laugh in mutual sympathy and stop so the animals or birds might collect themselves and flee. That environment was a North American deciduous forest we came to know as dangerous, exacting, stark, and yes, strangely alluring in its mysterious ways as the Chocolate Mountains. That covey of quail had never seen human beings either and its communal explosion of bird hotness and panic echoed into the thinning heat-waved patches of crumpled sun-ray. The lean remote fierceness of those quail reminded me of the wild turkey we came to know in another very distant world, the superbly intelligent birds scouring the stingy forest floors with their hard alert female scouts patrolling the edges and ready to die at any necessary second for their sisters and the young who were being taught to survive in that exacting world.

Friday November 12th 2005: Morning sky filled with cumulous clouds. Our walk around Lake Murray included sightings of heron, pelican, mallard, and cormorants that congregate on phone lines strung over the water each bird wrapped in duplicate stillness one next to the other. The previous week we watched a group of white pelicans moving in a communal ever enclosing circle, hunting and harvesting, each motion of wing and bill synchronized in a calm, flexed, deadly/rhythmically elegant bunching. Their final closure was in itself flower-like and folded on unremitting concentrations as other pelicans landed around this core; pelican feet touching water surface, spreading, the sound of that bird flesh touching water, so old, so imperviously persistent.

A headline this week unlike any I ever thought I'd see:

"White House working to defeat a Torture Ban"

and along with it an editorial today in the LA Times by David Gelernter entitled "When Torture is the Only Option":

> McCain is a bona fide hero. But there's nothing courageous in standing firm with virtually the whole cultural leadership of this nation and the Western world, under any circumstances. It is too easy. To take a principled stand that you know will make people loathe you and vilify you – that's what integrity, leadership, and moral courage are all about. This time Cheney is the hero. McCain's taking the easy way out . . . We do not torture such terrorists to punish them. God forbid we should do as they do. But if torture (used with repugnance) can stop even one such atrocity, our duty is hideously plain . . .

The whole thing seems broken, sealed with darkness, savagery, murder-slippage into the precincts of grisly moral goods and their "hideously plain" promises. Is this blank plunge into the further commonalities of "repugnance" heart pus of the nation's breath – throat killing dictions and sneaky mind fever posing as competent rational or ordered public discourse? These years of baseness. We are all with the present "leaders" and with such public intellectuals as this "David Gelernter" as Olson said in his discussion of Melville " . . . leaning on a straw . . ."

Sunday November 13th 2005: 10:00am, 81 degrees, a magnificent day. We're preparing our gardens for the winter, spreading mulch, upturning soil, fertilizing. We also bought a new prefab vinyl storage building, something interesting for tools, ceramic supplies, other equipment and odds which surface for our needs. A chance to expand Gail's studio.
Daniel Schorr's commentary on NPR this morning was another chronicle of present sadnesses – the CIA's "Black Sites" where all the "Renditions" sink; the senate and house are in turmoil, not over the fact and existence

of these termination depots, but that "someone" leaked their reality and possible locations.

Tuesday November 15th 2005: 9:19am, 84 degrees. Our orange tree is producing its third crop this year! We're organizing and cleaning Gail's studio. A very strange piece involving torture in Iraq. U.S. soldiers apparently used Uday Hussein's "pet" lions to terrify detainees in July of 2003. One can speculate about the dictator's mad son – how many people were used as bait and entertainment for the cruel whims of this man – and can we not include our own mad sons and their use of these leftover monstrocities; the casual plunder of our whims, conquering logics touch screen integrated for the viciousness of what here is the American vision of the "Booth Visit" and its innovative interfaces honed to customized Zigguratic needs.

And as in Poland, so in Russia lying two centuries in its isolate past until the 1890s when more than a million Jews left those ancestral regions. The terrible depression of the century's last decade must have made the world look like a grass-fire seared snake. In Russia the folds of that reptile worked as of a consumption eating the peasants, eating them all down to the children. The Czar infecting each facet of his personal darkness let the darkness loose. And the peasantry swallowed the darkness, ate of its tufts, its thinnesses and hanged thousands of Jews for being (revolutionary) – let the secret police of its spectacularly veiled rulers come to them, exhaust them with breathless whispers, send them out dream drenched and sated to burn the homes and bones of Jews, rape the women, choke the men, crush the children in Baptism.

The "senate' votes today. The issue: whether Guantanamo detainees or non-citizens have the right to question the legality of their imprisonment (this equally applies to the immigrants coming from the other Americas).

A senatorial measure, passed last week would overturn the Supreme Court's ruling granting detainees the right to challenge their detention. Lindsay Graham of South Carolina, authored the language which would bar the detainees any access to the courts.

More, yet again, on the California prison system's health care crisis which is now on the verge of collapse. The conditions have worsened since U.S. District Court Judge, Thelton Henderson, placed the system in receivership in June of 2005. Men and women continue to die because of neglect, untreated diseases, infection, and filthy conditions.

Is the State without sanction of the courts, in these instances, engaged in murder? (it seems so simple a question to ask, but in asking it, what exhaustions, squalors, what indifferences and vast brokenness do we threaten to uncover in our lives?). If the ethics of the "Geneva Convention" – the ethics which remind any soldier (or nation) that one someday might and must return to daily life and the conduct which grounds daily life in life sustaining encounters not death sustaining encounters (which so ruthlessly impersonate daily existence) with individuals and communities, are seen as no more than the "quaint," if we are no longer capable of apprehending the immediate presences of these concerns (beyond their portrayal in American Democracy as nothing more than "product": Alberto Gonzales, author of the "quaint," testifying before a senate panel yesterday Aug. 2. 06, said of the Bush administration's new plan for prosecuting detainees, while still permitting the use of coerced confessions and preventing the accused from seeing classified evidence being used against them "I think the product we're considering now is better") then it seems that the release of domestic prisoners into daily "American" life encompasses a similar ethical void since those prisoners inside are being released into our formulations of neglect, contempt, and as carefully a designed an oblivion as our communal sicknesses can construct and imagine. This seems to me too only the most limited browse through ethical considerations but the loss of "Daily Life" and the ethical conditions of what makes "Daily Life" come alive have become the lowest and most despised of our shared stories. The vulgarity that erupts out of such superb dismissals is a politics that feasts upon cynical life weariness and soul nausea and no civilization that so feasts, to expand on Thomas Hardy's statement in "Tess of the D'Urbervilles" can expect to live. Our "War on Crime" is *the* war out of which all the other wars emerge. It is, as well, a war profits business and the groundwork of that business and its profits is to render "clientele" as useless, and, in the high minded formula of that reduction for the Keepers, to make the "useless" counterfeit for, any other, but the World of Corrections wherever that world might find its world-wide roots. Such *dying* then, as now occurs in California's prisons, cannot interfere with either security or punishment as the ruling ideals. Have we, in the face of this directive, come upon that moment in the constructs of our civilization so hauntingly envisioned in Blake's "The Four Zoas" when, wherever we might turn for succor in the former "gardens of wisdom," we find ourselves instead in "a field of horrid graves" so enrapt are we in the Treasures of Desolation?

"Call Our Criminal Justice Studios For More Information"

Wednesday November 23rd 2005: Prison officials in this state are actively lobbying for the execution of Stanley "Tookie" Williams. Attorneys for Williams say this official conduct is "dishonorable and contrary" to everything that justice in this country represents. A Fontana California chief of police has gone so far as to claim that a "Lafayette Jones" – a known sex offender wanted for raping a 13 year-old girl, is "Williams's son." Spokespersons for that police agency when confronted with this smear, its old/new horizons of marketing eugenic degeneracy, lynching hysterias, and bottomless fear of criminals/terrorists (even those chained down to state lethal injection platforms) said the reliability of the issue "really is irrelevant at this point..." America's latest business models in the quietudes and severities of their hate gilts demonstrating the expert fermentations of the venom and its excitements no matter what "proofs" are required for the destruction of the unfit.

And L.A. County jails full of escape prone prisoners. 20 this year and a city corrections department which handles up to 20,000 inmates a day. The number 20 so sacred to ancient America. The Count of Days. 20 as the basic "uinal" or the number system of 20 named days each one itself a living creature, fish-footed with dwarfs climbing its supportive columns to receive each morning the New Born Sky. How this number staggers a 21st century "American" population even though for the last three years 148,229 inmates have been given early release, serving only a fraction of their sentences. The cause: shortage of jail beds.

The following numbers record the period from July 2002 to December 2005:

Number of Inmates released early:	148,229
Rearrested:	15,775
Charged with Robbery:	518
Charged with Assault:	1,443
Charged with a Sex Offense:	215
Charged with Murder:	16

The crimes were committed during the period the offenders were supposed to have been serving their sentences. But because of the crisis of jail space in this three-and-a-half year horizon sheriff's officials have disregarded sentences handed down by the courts and, in some instances, let inmates go free even though specific judges instructed that those individuals must serve their full sentences. The L.A. County sheriff, Lee Baca, has defended his decision of early release as a "last resort" because of budgetary cuts even though such releases place innocent citizens in significant danger of being harmed. Those who have murdered during the period of their supposed sentences have done irreparable damage and the relatives of the deceased are left in agonizing bewilderment over this fact.

One can pronounce the word "Blackmail" with the solidity of its six deri-
sive consonants and the fact that prison economics and the realities it initiates drowns us in ordeals that bear almost too uncanny a resemblance to
Blake's "white Dot" and the "way of the Devouring Power":

Having a white Dot calld a Center from which branches out
A Circle in continual gyrations, this became a Heart
From which sprang numerous branches varying their motions
Producing many Heads three or seven or ten, & hands & feet
Innumerable at will of the unfortunate contemplator
Who becomes his food : such is the way of the Devouring Power

This passage appears at the beginning of "Jerusalem: Chap: 2." I don't
know of any more accurate description of the demonic realm Blake knew
he was living through and that future populations might be forced to live
through. One grasps immediately how frightened Blake was of the
"Mighty Ones of the Earth" who "worship" such an entity and how lonely
his examination of the weavings of mass spells and the worship of Dread
even the constant aesthetizings of Dread as Dread drifts over the gyrations
of randomness and abandonment and that that aesthetics has become an
easy neighbor having no longer any need to hide its ancient stealth or its
loathsomeness. One sees the capacity for mass hypnosis preserved in the
urban life of the Americas from Tikal forward (though even more remote
evidence may be found in other so far unexcavated sites). The graffiti
scratched onto the palace walls of that great city portrays evidences of
mass conjurings and unsettling wonders American urban populations
seem to have been susceptible to for thousands of years. I don't know
exactly what Blake saw but I do consider it to be similar to that graffiti on
the walls of Tikal, something troubling and frightening about the human
experience in the urban Americas (because I think this passage extends
out of "America a Prophecy") someone had the courage to record. That
moment of such quiet scratchings dilates in our time and preserves what

instance of hallucination or pitch of intensely shared arousals and longing we cannot pretend to know, but its existence, nonetheless, is a profound sort of fingerprint (similar to the sudden appearance of a mammoth footprint on the walls of an arroyo in the Anza Borrego Wastes) that holds both curiosity and foreboding over what so peculiarly throbs in this recording.

Used to be, in the time of the Grandmothers, that the things of the forest came once in a while for a race. "Bet yew," they'd say, make themselves in flames no camp fire'd ever seen. "Choose one'a yerselves. Yew win. Yew git ta kill tin'a us. Lose. We git a thousand a'yours." Sometimes all that was left of a whole people was six, maybe seven sons. Only a daughter. Couldn't figure a way to stop themselves from loving those races. Who's to say, after all, which meat is which as you row the coasts of the Fresh Water Seas. The curves never come to an end there. Nobody knew about the rules over form. Who gets to be what and goddamnit stay stuck there. Don't be straying into apparition. Begin the murdering all over again.

Friday November 25th 2005: Yesterday we had a Thanksgiving picnic at a state park in East County. The area covered by chaparral and huge outcrops of granitic boulders, some over 30 storeys high, a plateau overlooking the Anza Borrego Wilds and the partial curvature of the planet extending into the mountainous terrain of Northern Baja. An extraordinary desert silence along with very blue pollution free sky which, in the late afternoon, presented not only the Sun's descent but the shadow of the Earth rising and mixing with the paling darkening tones of blues, purples, pinks, and whitish lights of fallen gorgeous night.

Gail's mother, Ora, died after an eight-year struggle from late-stage Alzheimer's disease

Monday November 28th 2005: Spent the weekend straightening, cleaning studios, readying for more stages of preparation for Gail's one person show in the spring. Gail off to her hometown of Kingston, New York to see to the arrangements of her mother's funeral with her sisters.

Tuesday November 29th 2005: 9:00am, 63 degrees. Cool nights and spectacular starry skies. Orion, the Pleiades, Mars, Venus, Saturn, Jupiter on their great journeys.

Wednesday November 30th 2005: 8:30am, 68 degrees. Crows squawking, oranges ripening to a sweetness on the vine and these cold nights of stars and planets are remarkable.
A warden at Lancaster State Prison has been removed from his position after officials learned that "a sexually explicit comedy performance containing racially offensive material was presented last year ..." The prisons are the states' and the nation's undermining wounds where racism and hatred are constantly fermented and refined and allowed to become the finest vintages; calibrated destitutions to be poured at the will of the Keepers inside/outside devouring any movement toward health.

A Mojave real estate scheme conjured by my father and his Hollywood friends. A thing downslope from the high wire nudist camps of the old Cajon Summit, set out on that desolation like *The* Primeval Tape Worm itself, now enrooted on the hills, in the canyons, quivering with the ungratified lineaments of its newly born howling infinities, Mother of the Body of Death.

Army Colonel, Ted Westhusing, a military ethicist from West Point, has committed suicide in apparent despair over the war profits industries. "In an e-mail to his family, Westhusing seemed especially upset by one conclusion he had reached: that traditional military values such as duty, honor, and country had been replaced by profit motives in Iraq, where the U.S. had come to rely heavily on contractors for jobs done by the military . . ." Does it matter that one man who represents the military at so crucial a level who does actually look at and examine this war gets driven to oblivion? (Does this suicide relate to the present uncovering, today Aug. 3rd. 06, involved with the investigation of the 101st Airborne Division's 3rd Brigade and the 'atmosphere" created by Col. Michael Steele and his officers that allowed excessive violence by encouraging "kill counts," illegal orders to shoot Iraqi men of "military age," and tolerating violent anti Arab racism in the Samarra murders?) And what sort of victim is Ted Westhusing, sunk beyond sorrow or madness or sanity itself? Is it the face of Melville's pock-headed Elijah, shimmering in blood pools of the Tigris, that Mesopotamian trickle for us, now more boundless than any fate-devouring Pacific? Does such an easily overlooked incident as this one matter? Does it matter that a high ranking military officer at the moment of his most profound loneliness who teaches the difficult questions about war and violence and Democracy to generations of Army officers upon seeing the evil of his Nation's actions does not want to breath one more instant of the rottenness he sees? How are we to regard Homer's terrifying "watchfires" and what they can no longer illuminate; neither the delicate feasting of dogs that can afford the choicest cuts so much death and sorrow has to offer, or Pound in the Envoi facing the catastrophic results War and what it means to even attempt to think about those results, the waiting disfigurements of mind and heart wrote:

> Died some pro patria, non dulce non et decor
> walked eye-deep in hell
> believing old men's lies, then unbelieving
> came home, home to a lie,
> home to many deceits,
> home to old lies and new infamy . . .

And what infamy now resides in each of our homes? Can an answer be found to this question through a military psychologist's response to Colonel Westhusing's case. Lt. Col. Lisa Breitenbach wrote:

> Despite his intelligence, his ability to grasp the idea that profit is an important goal for people in the private sector was surprisingly limited . . .

Is Ms. Breitenbach the "Elsie" of William Carlos Williams's great poem, one of the "Pure Products of America"

expressing with broken

brain the truth about us – -

Her implication that Colonel Westhusing's horror over war profits greed is a pathology before the rightful healthy profit goals of the private sector tells us how barren the nuclear fires have made us; that those fires as we supposed in our nightmares were hot and they were not and we are frozen in their hostility far more than we are willing to or can admit. We are not melted or incinerated with grief before our evils rather we have a cool sardonic vigor that summons us to the glacial fruits our wars offer us

As does politics:

Alice Notley says in her "Disobedience"

the longer change takes, the more
there is to forgive
Until one has no interest in forgiveness

or until the Spider Stones of the ancient American cities open their portals that have been closed for thousands of years to what reawakened fate? The primeval basic work of making the whole visible and invisible world livable for every creature; what it seems a god or gods ask human beings to do as First Act of any day (remembering Sunrise is the most political moment) human beings no longer can or want to do. We have used the Cloud of Ch'ulel, the "soul stuff" out of which reality is composed. I often think that our acquifirs and reservoirs of oil are also a part of the Ch'ulel Cloud upon which we have feasted without once having asked what will happen when the Ch'ulel is no longer; and is Ms. Breitenbach's "evaluation" a fact by which we can gauge the loss of awe in our lives. In this I recall Henry James's great challenging question for me as a novelist and how I regard the writing of such forms:

What is the most developed degree of Being thinkable?

The great dreamer asks and adds to the furthering resonances of the question:

The active, contributive, close-circling wonder which provides distinction, provides vitality and variety

"Once any people becomes this hungry, wants not just the flesh, but the whole dream of having ever lived . . ." and he remembered his lover stopped on the motion of the final verb saying no more other than to stroke his newly bearded cheek as they rode their horses past a stand of creek bottom cottonwoods. Somewhere in that immobile haze, he thought, of butchery and fury and empty-handed despair risen like some pearl to embrace whatever sees it or hears it is a breath reserved for the Children of the Ravished, as if they were an inventory waiting crazily to be counted in the master-nights where mercy out of which Buffalo Bill constructed his arbitrary masses of the strange, the bewildered ensembles curving, dares not come.

Monday December 5th 2005: Mars. Once a planet with ancient reservoirs of ice "but no water" as the new portraits reveal. Earliest Mars far different from previous speculations over a possible manufactured second Earth of new colonial oxygenated utopias. Though water may have once flowed on its surfaces leaving evidence of huge fossil water falls Mars underwent a drastic transformation at least 3.5 billion years ago. The planet "fell dry" (the words used by the presiding astrogeologists). The waiting celestial Virgin of off planet urges revealed as a skeleton of this world.

The secret Pentagon program that pays Iraqi newspapers to publish information favorable to the U.S. mission (contracted through the Lincoln Group) and the U.S. military information operations task force in Baghdad has committed "transgressions."

"Transgressions" are propaganda masked as news or advertisements or lies presented as truthful information. Lawrence DiRita, special assistant to Donald Rumsfeld acknowledged that "no one knew specifically how the Lincoln Group contract was being executed in the Iraq . . . There wasn't anyone who was sufficiently knowledgeable to deconstruct this particular contract . . ." DiRita said. The person who will "deconstruct" all that appears or disappears however is senator John Warner who presided over and erased Abu Ghraib from primary public consciousness or conscience and who will preside over this "inquiry" smothering it in equal silence (has anyone heard about the issue as I complete this manuscript on Wednesday June 14th 2006). The Pentagon's manipulation of events and information may be equal to and even surpass Abu Ghraib. The long lasting harms initiated by this deceit, the baseness, the construction of a purposeful foundation of peril calls up the strange vowel of King Lear, in the "Fools" apprehension of World/Loss enveloped by Word/Loss not as artifice but lived dimension:

Now thou art an O without a figure

The whole blankness falling onto dog hungers and fragilities; juniper almost and the blossoms of yucca accompanied by a She who bites the tongues of human-faced bulls on the farthest shores of the galaxy Lordship of Sippar the inscription continues though the sum of a king may be 28,000 years the sum of a shepherd after a king may be a thousand sickened cities.

The Lincoln Group's web site reads:

> A strategic Communications & Public Relations Firm providing insight & influence in challenging & hostile environments across a wide variety of issues, from governance to economic development, our professionals work every day of the year in some of the most inhospitable environments in order to get your message communicated effectively . . .
>
> Our professionals often work in foreign communities where crime, insurgency, terrorism, extreme poverty and instability make communications and operations an extreme challenge. So, people often wonder "How can you work there?" It's not so simple, but we rely on our experience, quality people, flexibility, and low profile to get the job done. The bottom line to our success often comes down to the fact that we live and work inside these communities. Our staff members are experts on the communities they work in and are able to immerse themselves in them unobtrusively. This level of intimacy allows us greater insight and ensures that our teams always have their finger on the pulse of local perceptions and behaviors . . .

This prose with its pornographic suggestions of "intimacies" and "fingers" on pulses of various "behaviors" and "perceptions" reeks of the vulgarities enshrined in Vegas limousine ads and secret police anthropology. "Pigtails and Panties" for instance announces:

I'm stronger than I look and I'm looking to discipline you . . .

and "Barely Turned Legal" coos:

I'm built like a rock . . .

There's Francine who likes "beef jerky"
Bobby with a specialty of "Thanksgiving Dinners"
Stacy who likes to have someone read "good books" to her
Taylor whose preference is "green eyes"
Heidi who dislikes "final exams"
And Candy who is "sticky"

This prose is closely matched to the advertisements one sees for the prison industrial complex. The mirrorings are not random nor is the interchangeability of malevolence in terms of the evolution of a permanently infected daily life in America:

MCI wipes out one of the highest crime areas in America.
MCI Maximum Security is the toughest and most ambitious system of controlling inmate calling in America. It bring the power of the mainframe right into your prison. And it sentences every other system of preventing illicit telephone use to obsolescence.
MCI Maximum Security is mainframe based to give you total control over calls made out of your prison. Now you can scrutinized frequently called numbers quickly and efficiently. So illicit call forwarding schemes, credit card scams and subscription fraud can be detected much earlier than before.
And with centralized call blocking at your fingertips, you can stop a call when you want it stopped . . .

The sense of "sticky" identities applies to what was once known as "Iraqex LLC" in 2004 and then became the "Lincoln Group" in 2005. In June of 2005 the "Lincoln Group" was "awarded" a five year $100 million dollar Global Support Contract by the United States Special Operations Command. (What was it Conrad said accompanies any mass of lies, "a taint of death" the rotted bite of the whole thing; one could be embarrassed by the central noun but I don't know of another that contains the burden).

In the summer of 2005 an MCI scheme was exposed in New York State's prisons. MCI was imposing rates of 600% above normal for calls made from inside. The profit share for New York State was $20 million on the basis of the majority of calls made to prisoner's homes. Such calls are often the only lifeline individuals might have and those 600% rate hikes fall on prisoners' families and communities. The innovation those hikes provide are the unmentioned doublings of punishment which also "spread" like democracy in Iraq intimately, flexibly immersed in frequent scrutiny (did the superbly punishment administered criminal class inform its twin superbly protection administered criminal class and is this the prodigious work of the Arrival and its arcades of promised strangulations?).

New Orleans: The soils washed in with the Floods of Katrina are being deciphered. Gina Solomon, who lead the research team, said, "Residents could become ill by inhaling or touching contaminated sediments. Long-term risks could include cancer, neurological disease, and reproductive system ailments."

Is it the Hanging Goddess of the earlier cities, the:

Ix Tab germinating
water
will be death

teeth first
nostrils halfway
gulped
as if
of
one sky?

Tuesday December 6th 2005: 10:30am, 79 degrees: A beautiful morning and accompanying crisp nights with a spectacular presence of stars and planets. The sunsets are stunning with the Moon and Venus rising as twins and escorts of blossoming cactus night flowers with their uncanny fascinations and lures.

Before the tragic, stumbling, misery of "policy" Bush administration spokesman, Donald Rumsfeld, is throwing a veil of optimism.

Serpent milk of the Cadavers
let loose

The Harvest:
          It will have pain in it
          will not trouble
          even those who sow it

"Love the World – and stay inside it
               Concentrate ..."

Olson says.

What would happen if the Courage Givers along with their Art were to completely wither away in this time of witherings? It is possible. The Work. The Generosity. The Care is no more nor less mortal than the Breathers who Breathed it in this time of fragilities.

Wednesday December 7th 2005: 9:31am, 74 degrees, though at night the temperatures drop to the low 40s. Mild Santa Ana winds and the clarity of the atmosphere allows the day shadow of the Earth to rise partially toward the vanishing point of the horizon and one can see far to the coastal plains and the mountains hovering in the East. These wonders gather and offer a daily grace.

There is small passage in William H. Brewer's "Up and Down California." The author had been climbing in the still extensively unexplored region of Lake Tahoe and Carson Pass in 1863-64:

> The view is the grandest in this part of the Sierra. On the east, four thousand feet beneath, lies Lake Tahoe, intensely blue; nearer are about a dozen little alpine lakes, of very blue, clear, snow water. Far in the east are the desolate mountains of Nevada Territory, fading into the indistinctness in the blue distance. South are the rugged mountains along the crest of the Sierras, far south of Sonora Pass – a hundred peaks spotted with snow. All along the west is the western slope of the Sierra, bathed in a blue haze and smoke; and beyond lies the great plain, which for 200 miles of its extent looks like an ill-defined sea of smoke. Above which rise the dim outlines of the coast ranges for 150 miles along the horizon, some of them over 150 miles distant ...

California at this point, from 1849 to the early 1860s, had already been significantly ravaged, but one could still report, as Brewer does, of being able to see for hundreds of miles depending on elevation, winds, and seasons. In his descriptions of the Los Angeles Basin at the beginning of the book, the author/geologist records being able to see from the highest foothills of the San Gabriel Mountains the looming reflections of the San Diego Bay to the south, and to the north, the outlines of Point Conception. This is a radius of approximately 200 hundred miles. The prose is unpretentiously clear, active, and generative in terms of the author's awe for what he sees and feels and as primary witness knowing the War of his time lies on those most distant edges, ready with its barrenness and dread, he gives us a way to locate our disconnected "future" in relationship to the reality of the "Sky" or what once could have been identified as *the* "Sky" unfolding in expanses which no longer exist. Passages like this might offer us a way to actually inhabit the Injury to the World we have created and been born into much more carefully, though this time, only 142 years in a not apparently distant past, is so dimly remote, that any ability to call it up seems feeble and exhausting in the forward press of accumulation that ignobly closes in with frenzies small and large whose impassive unrealities corrode and extend the mystery of our remove. A small, terribly obscure "passage" like this one can have the power to "appall" the Soul, as Blake asks his reader to let the word settle under blood, to grow pale in Death and dismay, and to regard what this poet saw as the only alternative, the only vision for any future; "War's Overthrow" no matter what its guise.

"War" in the poet's examination becomes even more intensely complicated. The contraries of Innocence and Experience are further enframed in "Jerusalem: Chapter 2, PLATE 38" with its frightening vision of "Heavens & Hells conglobing in the Void." This "Void" devours equally both Heavens and Hells where the inhabitants of those worlds remain

> Brooding in holy hypocritic lust, drinking the cries of pain
> From howling victims of Law . . .

The "Heavens" which are constructed out of this "Void" and its laws Blake calls:

> Swelld & bloated General Forms, repugnant to the Divine-
> Humanity . . .

whose world belongs to "sympathy" "love" "benevolence" and the protection of the "minute particulars" or the ground out of which Imagination, Soul, and "identity" are formed. Blake in this passage mixes his Bardic Furies with the quietudes of his immediate attentions to present things and in his creation of a moment of crisis and threshold drops every pretence of reference and description in order to form and deform error into evolving elements of recognition:

> But here the affectionate touch of the tongue is closd in by deadly teeth
> And the soft smile of friendship & the open dawn of benevolence
> Become a net & a trap. & every energy rendered cruel,
> Till the existence of friendship & benevolence is denied:
> The wine of the Spirit & the vineyards of the Holy-One,
> Here: turn into poisonous stupor & deadly intoxication:
> That they may be condemnd by Law & the Lamb of God be slain:
> And the two Sources of Life in Eternity, Hunting and War
> Are become the Sources of dark & bitter Death & of corroding Hell . . .

This kind of passage brings me into contact with the Crisis of Beginnings and the rapturous suspicions Blake audaciously dilates. By this one is instantly drawn once more to the Paleolithic Caves and the narratives still held in those darknesses. Are they addresses to "Hunting and War" as Blake imagines and if that is their Truth then does it render for us with shattering exactitude our participations willing or unwilling in stupors and intoxications which indicate how drastically We and the "Sources" have been transformed? Having read this poetry for 35 to 40 years I am still drawn to and terribly frightened by the Artist/Poet's patient, tense study and what it seems to locate. The words exist on the page not so much as a poetic line but as twentieth century "assemblage," Blake striking out in these dimensions of syllable and tone toward a kind of "Merzbau" never experienced in poetry and which call to the legendary forms of Kurt Schwitters's "The Cathedral of Erotic Misery" as one re-imagines "The Marriage of Heaven & Hell" as a spreading hearth fire into the house of Blake's later works.

This also Pearl Harbor Day. My mother's brother manned a machine gun in those hours as the Zeros dive bombed. Then he was sent on another journey of "island hopping" from Guadalcanal to Kwajalein to Tarawa and beyond. He went in as beautiful young boy and came back a malarial, nightmare haunted man for the rest of his life. He was a participant, in addition, in an American foray prior to the Japanese attack that has nearly disappeared from "Story" whatever "Story" might be in this time. He and a brigade of other young men were sent to patrol the jungles edging the Panama Canal. The fear at that moment of still well groomed American isolation was that the Japanese would invade Panama. 90% to 95%, as I remember my earliest childhood narratives, of those men were killed by the poison frog darts of the Indians extending the colonial nightmares of the sixteenth century to the second stagings of World War in the twentieth as the depths of the New World still erupted on those young soldiers who may as well have been carrying the smells of the Nina, the Pinta, or the Santa Maria in their corpse pale hoverings, initial visions of the cruel and "mighty Polypus" "growing over the whole Earth": a new pornography whose scale, as Blake attempts to give it relation and distinction, to define its "embryon" no matter how damaging to himself finds startling extension in Rimbaud, Thomas Pynchon's "Vineland," Fanny Howe's "Nod" and the opening passages in J. G. Ballard's "Crash":

I think now of the other crashes we visualized, absurd deaths of the wounded, maimed and distraught. I think of the crashes of psychopaths, implausible accidents carried out with venom and self disgust, vicious multiple collisions contrived in stolen cars on evening freeways among tired office workers. I think of the absurd crashes of neurasthenic housewives returning from their VD clinics, hitting parked cars in suburban high streets. I think of the crashes of excited schizophrenics colliding head-on into stalled laundry vans in one-way streets; of manic-depressives crushed while making pointless U-turns on motorway access roads; of luckless paranoids driving at full speed into the brick walls at the ends of known cul-de-sac; of sadistic charge nurses decapitated in inverted crashes on complex interchanges; of lesbian supermarket manageresses burning to death in collapsed frames of their midget cars before the stoical eyes of middle-aged firemen; of autistic children crushed in rear-end collisions, their eyes less wounded in death; of buses filled with mental defectives drowning together stoically in roadside industrial canals . . .

Blake's infra-regioned, erotic, malevolently pulsing "white Dot" sprung in its motions and gyrations into production identities and body parts remains to this day untouched by the "Romantic cannon" of much of even the most advanced poetries claiming residence in this radicalism, and floats as one of the leviathans on the "Lake" (has it become the Sea?) of his "Udan Adan" and its "Flood." And the "sociochasm" to use Charlie Steins's word "branches out/ a Circle . . ." Further, if one looks at Blake's watercolor, "Satan Exulting over Eve" 1795, the sense of a drastically erotic intensity and its amplitudes of carnality, abandonment, enriched fatality, transport, and wondrously unveiled threat his contrary states of the soul must have if the soul is to stay alive, one, at the same time, discerns this watercolor's connection to the conditions of personal intimacy so susceptible to the "system" Blake reveals in "PLATE 11" of "The Marriage of Heaven and Hell" having to do with the ancient names, adorations, and enlargements

Homo Sapiens seem to have undergone a 100,000 to 150,000 years ago when they began to leave evidences of their respect for the transience of which they were anonymously and inescapably a part. The great "naked" license of this water color combined with Goya's "They Already Have Seats" (Los Caprichos, No., 26, 1793-96) may be the first forays into the merchandized weapons-ready landscapes of the present, poised in their enigmatic warnings, subtleties, and suggestions for Imaginative alternatives (Does "reality" or the "present" as we've come to experience it have the skin of a "stealth bomber": can language in its present guises any longer detect it or has language itself become a part of the mysterious "Hermaphroditic Condensations" Blake refers to in "PLATE 58" of "Jerusalem"? Can the artist begin to Imagine new forms of Courage, Curiosity, and Wonder in this time with the help of the advanced reassessments archaeology, paleontology, and genetics make available?).

Thursday December 8th 2005: 10:15am, 72 degrees. Overcast. Our new crop of oranges is ripening. The process seems to be continual. The tree can't stop and we wonder if this is further, more intimate, backyard symptom of the planetary changes.

Condalezza Rice failed yesterday to clarify the U.S. view on torture. As further clarification of intent Bush wants to expand detention space on the Border, build new holding pens for "illegal immigrants": the space of industrial punishment having no limit if properly perceived as mineral wealth. Central Houselessness of the Nation and vice-principles of these frenzies. Silence in the "empty spaces of America" Lawrence saw as "still unutterable, almost cruel" no longer "empty": transformed into "holding facilities" "headcount location systems" "audio and visual alert control stations" time tagged, litigated, node utilized body units which transform even the most legitimate sorrows into detached imbecilities:

great woe of human unworthiness

as Lawrence felt its soundings carrying humanity forward into what?

To remind the unweary about how beauty can be almost as peculiar as a country cemetery where the ghosts weave the stems of their wildest onions into straw hats, knowing that though Death has delivered them completely, the manners of fashion even there might still bring on an invisible smile

Saturday December 11th 2005:The "Tookie Williams" case locally has become a racist carnival and infection. A right wing radio talk venue, "The John and Ken Show" KFI am, 640, one of the most popular in Southern California, has become a personal lobby for the death of this man. As his time moves closer the former CRIP has become the target for the show's hosts, John Kobyet and Ken Chiampou, who have been devoting their 3 to 7 prime time rush hour presentation to their "Tookie Must Die for Murdering Four Innocent People" campaign announced with a recording of four gunshots. The broadcasts have included one of the hosts reading Williams's "Gangs and Drugs" book in an affected street accent, mocking the speech rhythms of African Americans.
A name that arises: James Cameron, now nearly lost to White America, the only survivor of the last recorded lynching of Black men to have taken place; Marion, Indiana, 1930. A huge night mob called out his and the names of his two friends, Thomas Shipp and Abe Smith who were dragged out of their jail cells, kicked, bit, beaten, and hung.

Sunday December 12th 2005: A lovely morning. The Santa Anas push our wind chimes. Gail's new ceramic pieces are presences which strike at the core of supposed "identity" and what assumptions might accompany such imperatives and "faith in form." The pieces are "portraits" faceless, and in that, starkly and mysteriously monumental in their ability to hold reservoirs of emotion and what Robert Duncan called the wonderful and terrible trouble of an art that draws the viewer toward both a comic and sexually luring unease and the haunted disturbances which allow the work its vigorous, enthralling freshness.

We walked the promenade and pier of Pacific Beach. Went to watch a run of 15 to 20 foot waves. The force of the swells caused the pilings to sway as we saw both board and body surfers try to manage the heavy, sheer break of these huge sections lit up in the late afternoon by a jade-like green sheen spreading over the ocean surface for miles into the low horizon. Waves of this size snap and build and hover in their convulsion and fury; their sound ripples over your facial skin and leaves its wild print somewhere in the self.

Tuesday December 14th 2005: 9"50am, 65 degrees. Arnold Schwarzenegger has allowed "Tookie" Williams to die. In his four page explanation the weight lifter cites a list of persons in the dedication to one of Williams's books, elaborating why he objects to the inclusion of a "killer" named George Jackson. Is the inspiration of George Jackson the true and final reason why Williams was executed?
The small remorseless savageries constantly fertilized by the Death Penalty and which shred the Lungs of the Nation.

Thursday December 16th 2005: 10:10am, 59 degrees. Overcast.
    An ancient Mayan mural has been discovered at San Bartolo, Guatemala. The fresco is nearly 2,100 years old. The site remote, at least a two day

hike from Tikal. The discovery supports the fact that the social structures for any culture of the Maya Classic Period, extending from AD 300 to AD 900, were actually in place at a much earlier date. Indigenous Peoples began farming the San Bartolo area around 700BC and started constructing a plaza and pyramids 300 years later. The city never became powerful and was mostly abandoned by AD 100. The mural is 30 feet long and accompanied by texts. The great Mayanist, David Freidel, rightly identified the painting as a "masterpiece" and further states, " . . . the scenes are executed with confidence, compositional imagination, and technical perfection of an artist who, while anonymous, must rank with the best the world has ever known . . ."

Robert Creeley, in the last reading I saw him give, said if he had a wish for the fate of his work, it would be the possibility that any of the poems might finally be the words themselves, and the author's name erased by the oblivions that wait for and finally name us all. The joining of the Life and Death Streams and the anonymous evidences wherever they may be found that might tell the story of our having been and wanting to be fully alive. I remember an interview Bob had sometime in the late 60s or early 70s, discussing his admiration for Lawrence and a line from "The Plumed Serpent" he had committed to his immediate grasp, "Living, I want to depar. to where *I am*."

In California $6 billion dollars a year is designated for the prisons. The stagnant number and its invisible costs never stops growing.
No monies are designated for jobs or job training in the inner cities where democracy might matter most to counter-act the feeder systems of social disintegration.
In 2004 93,000 youths between the ages of 18 and 24 dropped out of school with no jobs or job opportunities.
The number of drop outs for this same age group on a state-wide basis: 638,000.

1400th Chapter

Here the name of the Mothers, eye doctors
        burns from water flowers

        Crazy was seeing
        Dizzy was hearing

        and had no existence
        it was clear

        Brains and dripping rain

        Ordaining it was said

        Snatched face of Sun
        Tips of a billion tongues
        Rise of Gods
        or Hells

        It was as if the heart wandered
        after its two missing fingers

Sunday December 18th 2005: Cold night. Walked around Lake Murray this
morning. The white pelicans so unusual in their shapes and their bird
weight mixing air to water to feather.

An ancient city in the present nation of Syria has been excavated and examined. Tell Hamoukar was attacked more than 5,500 years ago. The archaeologists speculate the aggressor state may have been Uruk which dominated this region for at lest 2,000 years before the rise of the Babylonians and Assyrians. The destruction of Tell Hamoukar even at this early date bears all the marks of the violences so familiar to ourselves and, more startlingly, the purpose seems the establishment of the "world's earliest colonial system" stated archaeologist, Guillermo Algaze of UC San Diego. Algaze also added, "What makes it fascinating is it's so modern. Change the name and change the time period and we could be discussing European colonialization of the New World 500 years ago . . ."

There were stone and ceramic "balls" found everywhere, evidence of heavy destruction and force. The walls and buildings suffered extensive damage. The mark of the "City" in the late cycles of species evolution and with it the will to organize goulish murder from this moment nearly eight thousand years ago when the skills of carpentry, masonry, plant and animal domestication, organized conformity mixed with militarism and greed which from this evidence, seems already to have been in long practice. The pathology or the pathogen that sets it in motion; what is the forensic detail which might tell us of the relation of this evidence to a possible medical catastrophe which may have taken place between 15,000BC and 9,000BC shattering the previous brain chemistry of the species and initiated the sensations of pleasure attuned to the dreams of spectacular morbidity leading to the present civilian Iraq Body Count which must be included in this long awaited post-mortem of Tell Hamoukar? The number 30,000 more or less Bush's aides downplay as an 'unofficial" addition based on "public estimates" but what "public" exactly is not mentioned unless it is the ghost public of Uruk, something about "the women who choke lions" and how to erase their rebellion from memory.

Les Roberts of Johns Hopkins University School of Public Health led a team of researchers who examined the death rates of Iraq before and after the 2003 invasion, and, by making "conservative assumptions" based on

those death rates concluded "about 100,00 excess deaths" for women, children, and men have occurred in the months since. "Most" Roberts said, " . . . are attributable to breakdowns of the healthcare system prompted by the invasion while violent deaths have risen twentyfold . . ."
These findings, published in the respected British Medical Journal, the "Lancet," caused a firestorm of criticism.
In only 18 months the United States is responsible for fully ⅓ of the total number (1,300,000) of those murdered by Saddam Hussein's tyranny over a 30 year period.
The velocity of Democracy's "Heat Shadow" moving toward its "Chimney." (It is August 3 2006 as I frame and edit this material. The Bush administration has been unable to censor the numbers. The "Official" civilian death toll compiled by the Iraqi Health Ministry and other agencies is 50,000. Though the Health Ministry acknowledged an "undercount" the number in terms of comparative populations is the equivalent to 570,000 Americans "killed in three years").

Mars apparently lost its global magnetic field at least 3 billion years ago when its core solidified. In spite of that, the planet has hundreds of auroras which appear only in the ultra violet spectrum. The same phenomena appear on Earth when charged particles from the Sun strike the planet's protective magnetic shield which is generated by the Earth's revolving metal core. How hostile and biologically foreign Mars is will be tested by the first colonies of prisoners or other populations caught wandering into surplus. Is Mars a mummy waiting to be brought out of its sleep by the late phase plutocracy of our civilization and its "Off Planet" cults?

The California prison system is now supposedly phasing out its policy of segregating every in-coming prisoner by race. Racial segregation has been officially sanctioned in the system, so that the past and present suffer a reversal in order to guarantee the continued growth of the product based upon previous models of despair, but what can be defined now no longer as "despair" but assemblages of refined collapse which with scrutiny, guidance, and custom precision renders Justice itself as the most malicious agency stalking these populations.

Wednesday December 21st 2005: The Solstice and reports of more 20 foot waves.

Sunday January 1st 2006: Mixed Clouds and sun, 68 degrees. Walked around Lake Murray this morning after visiting Clay and Sarah in New York.

We attended a lovely and gentle New Year's celebration last night at Hiromi and Harold's. Sipped noodles for Long Life with dear friends.

First bird sighting for the New Year. An osprey circling a shallow Lake Murray outlet filled with white pelicans. Skies swept clean by the new rains!

WITHDRAWN
No longer the property of the
Boston Public Library.
Sale of this material benefits the Library